ALIKE REGARDLESS

This is Where it Began

With a Foreword by **Mark M. Bello**, Award winning author, Attorney, and Social Justice Advocate

YVENER DUROSEAU

Copyright © 2021 Yvener Duroseau

All rights reserved.

No part of this book may be used or reproduced in any manner whatsoever without written permission except in the case of brief quotations embodied in critical articles or reviews.

Published by 7 CHECKLIST ITEMS, LLC

ISBN: 978-1-7372969-0-4 (paperback)

ISBN: 978-1-7372969-1-1 (epub)

Name: Yvener Duroseau, Author

Title: Alike Regardless: This is Where it Began

Description: Tulsa Oklahoma, USA: Alike Regardless, 2021

Identifiers: LCCN | ISBN: 978-1-7372969-0-4 (pbk) |

ISBN: 978-1-7372969-2-8 (hbk) | ISBN: 978-1-7372969-4-2 (epub) |

ISBN: 978-1-7372969-6-6 (audiobook) |

Subjects: | Violence in Society (Books)| Social Work (Books)| Criminology (Books) | Education (Books)| Schools & Teaching (Books)| Education Theory (Books)| Social Justice (Books)| Activism (Books)

Classification: LLC 2021910632 (print)

Printed in the United States of America

This book is dedicated to my father Ilestdieu Duroseau. Everything that I am and everything that I hope to be, I owe to my father. He was to me a model man.

I also dedicate this book to every person that has experienced any type of discrimination and injustices. It is my hope that one day we will live in a world where everyone will be treated the way our creator intended for us to treat each other; as HUMAN. I hope this book will help you begin your healing process.

Plot Summary
The human race is unique!

Despite our many differences; religion, beliefs, race, skin color, or personal prejudices, there is still one thing that holds our world together, which is 'We are all human.'

However, we fail to see the beauty in the uniqueness of humankind, because we have been blinded by hate, bigotry, envy, and fear. We let hatred rule us, envy divide us, and fear keep us from fixing the mess. But it is time to wake up and see that everyone was created equal, perfect, and no different.

People have been born into unequal circumstances, which often leads them to make choices, which may either be good or bad, but one thing remains. We are still the same regardless. You may be asking, '...how can that be?'

This book will help you discover how there are no differences.

Hello there! No matter your skin color, race, gender, economic rank, sexual identity, or social status, we are human before anything else. In our diversities, we can still achieve oneness. Hatred may have ripped us apart, but there is still a way to mend the tear if only we can fix ourselves first, letting the uniqueness of the human race reflect inward and then to the outside, healing the human race. We should mend the tear and do it now! This book will be a guide.

About the Author

Yvener Duroseau is a renowned diversity and inclusion motivational speaker and consultant, digital marketing entrepreneur, creative writer, and published author who lives by discipline, confidence, strong social awareness, and mindful listening — traits that serve him well in all his noble pursuits.

This Haiti-born American grew up learning Haiti's profound history as the first nation in which a group of enslaved Africans came together to fight for and win back their independence. His book, *Alike Regardless*, is the first of many achievements he proudly wears like a badge of honor.

Alike Regardless, challenges humankind's internalized division. It issues a call to arms to readers to recognize humanity's beauty and uniqueness and take off the blinders of bigotry and hate.

Duroseau wrote his book to create a safe, productive space wherein he puts onto paper his genuine passion for a more diverse and socially just world. His professional insights and determination are palpable on every page and have succeeded in reaching out to readers, prompting them to think more deeply.

When he's not writing, speaking, consulting, or running his business, Duroseau spends his time in silence, voraciously reading books or consuming inspirational and motivational content. He is also an avid supporter and participant of the *Diligent Act of Love for Haiti* (DALOVE), a non-profit organization advocating for and supporting the education of underprivileged Haitian children. DALOVE helps kids reach their full potential and become an asset to their community and country.

Duroseau holds a Bachelor's degree in Health Care Management and an Associate's degree in Business Administration from Hodges University in Naples, Florida. He also has over seven years of management experience in numerous industries.

Duroseau also loves to travel and spend time with his wife, Kimberly, and their cat, Luna — his most devoted fans and constant support system as he works towards his goals.

Contents

Chapter Summary 8

Praises for *Alike Regardless* 13

Foreword 18

Chapter 1 This Is Where It Began 21

Chapter 2 Along Came Division 30

Chapter 3 The Motive Behind Divides 46

Chapter 4 Division Is Unfair 61

Chapter 5 The Home: Its Roots 80

Chapter 6 Love Heals All Wounds 96

Chapter 7 Love, The Hard Hill To Climb 109

Chapter 8 You Too, Have Value 124

Chapter 9 We Are Human 133

Chapter 10 The War Against Hate; A Final Call To Action 143

Bibliography 154

Acknowledgement 156

Chapter Summary

Chapter 1 - This is where it began

We will take a journey through the beginning of the separation and discrimination. This chapter will, through historical events, show that discrimination has lived with us right from the beginning of human existence. It is not a recent phenomenon and it has its genesis just as everything else does.

Chapter 2 - Along came division

We were all human before division came and pulled us apart. When division came, we seemed to forget the oneness in our humanity and focused on our weaknesses and differences. Division has caused greater harm than good to our society and we must all strive to fix the problem before it tears us apart.

Chapter 3 - The motives

Why divisions? Why would a human hate his fellow human? What makes it impossible for us to tolerate one another? We hear of gender wars, religious wars, racial wars, sexuality wars, etc. Why all these? Are they really necessary? What do we stand to gain in all of it? It is time to explore the reasons the human race is divided. This chapter will help to uncover the truth behind all these.

Chapter 4 - Division is unfair

We must not go on like this because we are all alike regardless. There is really no difference between us. We must learn to understand that even our differences are no differences at all. We did not create ourselves. No one made his/herself black or white, tall or short. Most of these things we have prejudices towards were naturally ordained by God. So why fight one another because of things we have no control over? We didn't choose our differences; therefore, divisions are unfair.

Chapter 5 - The home; its roots

They say charity begins at home. Everything starts from the home, even divisions. This chapter helps us learn how it is nurtured and fixes the problems right from within our homes. It is only by doing this that the change would be reflected in society. Everyone was brought up differently, and it most often affects our relationship with others outside our homes. So, here's how we can make sure these backgrounds are not fueling the divide.

Chapter 6 - Love heals all wounds

There is nothing greater than love, and this is what division lacks. A person would only spite or fight another when there is no love; therefore, love is paramount. Love heals all wounds and fixes all things. Love is what we need to mend the tear. But how can we really love one another? This chapter will teach us how.

Chapter 7 - Love, a hard hill to climb

As important as love is, it is also quite difficult to exhibit. It is easy to preach about love but in reality, living in love and by love is one of the most difficult things to do. But it gets easier when we try harder every day. Even if love is a hard hill to climb, we ought to climb this hill and learn to love if we truly intend to repair the division.

Chapter 8 - You too have value

We cannot fix the world if we do not fix ourselves first. If we do not value ourselves, no one would value us. We need to understand that we are not inferior like we may think we are. We are the same with everyone else. And just as we value ourselves, we should learn to value other people. Treating everyone respectfully and with value will help us abide in peaceful coexistence.

Chapter 9 - We are human

Yes, we are human, and we are human before anything else. Divisions shouldn't be, because we are alike regardless. The color of our skin or our religion doesn't have to matter.

The most important thing is that we all have blood running through our veins, which alone makes us have something in common. We share in this humanity, so let us embrace it.

Chapter 10- The call to action

It is time to wake up and act, learn to love, and not judge and mistreat people by our sentiments. We have learned everything about how the divide came to be and what we can do to fix it. Now is the time to do less talking and act it! It is now or never; we have to rise up and fight to keep that last piece of humanity. We are all it takes to bring the change we need. We should never let biases tear us apart; this is a call to action!

" We cannot solve our problems with the same thinking we used when we created them,"

Albert Einstein, Theoretical Physicist and The Nobel Prize in Physics

Praises for *Alike Regardless*

It's time to mend the tear. Join the movement
#Alikeregardless

"Courageous call to action! The author addresses human existence in pragmatic and academic ways supported by Bible verses. The division, love, and hate issues spun throughout the text to get the reader to self-exam and take actions to make the world better. Alike Regardless is a keeper!"- **Kenneth "MD" Madison** - Diversity & Inclusion Facilitator, MD Madison & Associates

"I devoured the first few chapters, feeling like Yvener was reading my mind! Alike Regardless stands out as a book to guide in facilitating conversations about human nature and introspection. I love the end-of-chapter questions and the message of hope that flows from the pages. This is a must-read for 2021 and beyond."- **Jessica Maronto** - Founder of SoLow Housing First

" As a thought leader in the DEI space, I truly appreciated the book as the author does an amazing job of walking the reader through the journey of how division has torn apart humankind. Then introduces love as the key to healing these wounds. I especially enjoyed the call to action, as it encourages everyone to take a stand and work together to fight for all human beings. I would highly recommend the book to anyone looking to understand better how hatred and bias have caused division in the world and learn what steps need to be taken to move forward as a society."- **Kerry D. Rosado** - CEO, Founder, Leadership & DEI Consultant Dyvergent Consulting Group, LLC

"I interviewed Yvener Duroseau and read his new book. This man is a breath of fresh air in a polluted social justice atmosphere. As my readers know, I am a fervent activist for social justice, and I get very frustrated with the slow pace of progress and the negativity of our rhetoric. But Yvener and his new book, "Alike Regardless," advance an absolutely contagious positivity! I highly recommend his book to anyone seeking to part ways with a hate-filled attitude. If you are a diversity advocate, buy this important book for someone who you know is not! This was a Zoom interview, but I wanted to hug this man when we said goodbye. If all of us adopted the demeanor and philosophies of Yvener Duroseau, the world would be a far better place." - **MARK M. BELLO** – Award Winning Author, Attorney and Social Justice Advocate

"Alike Regardless is both a portrait and a mirror of humanity's ideals! It is a reminder that we are all created by and in the image of our Creator. Amid the ever-growing cries against inequalities throughout the world, may Alike Regardless be both our mirror and guide in our pursuit of a perfect society." **- Jean G. Mathurin, M.D.,** Author of 7 Checklist Items for Success

"Alike Regardless is spectacular! It's a wake-up call for us to go back to being compassionate human beings again. Yvener gives us a blueprint to break down the walls that divide us. This book is a must-read regardless of the color of your skin." **- Rene Godefroy,** Award-winning Author of Kick Your Excuses Goodbye

"Wow! What an excellent and timely book! This is the book that the world needs right now. I work as a high school teacher at a small rural, mostly white school in Arkansas and the principles that you've outlined in your book are exactly what I try to teach my students. We are all human. We are all more alike than we are different. It starts when you are young. It's up to you to be kind and stand up for others to set an example. That is how we fix the racism problem. Parents have to instill in their children and young people have to step up and make the difference when it seems like no one else is listening. I really loved your book. So good!" - **Chelsea Burdick,** Historian & Educator

"The world needs more people like Yvener Duroseau, whose book, "Alike Regardless: This is Where it Began" offers hope and encouragement in a world that is beset with so much division, hate, and discord. Duroseau examines the root causes of division and encourages readers to remember that we are all human, all created equal, and that loving one another is so much better, so much more fulfilling than hate. The author recognizes that this is not easy, that it is hard to put aside long-held prejudices and feelings of distrust. But, he says, it is a hill worth climbing if we want to achieve a better world for all of humankind. Everyone who cares about others, about creating a better world, should read his book and share it with those who could use a little love as they relate to others." - **Bob Gatty** - Writer, Editor. Blogger. Political Commentator from NFN Radio News

"In the first chapter, I found myself being drawn into my own thoughts and questioning how I treat people. This book is very well written and challenges you on your views of equality, regardless of race or gender. It is a great resource for our current state of humanity." - **Patrick D. Thompson, MBA** - Talent Development Consultant at Lumen Technologies

HOW TO READ THIS BOOK

1. Don't read it.
   Consume it. Study it. Devour it.
   Treat it like a workbook - underline, highlight, circle, star, write, and put exclamation marks in the margins. Dog ear or put tabs on the pages and bits that have particular impact on you.
2. Answer the questions from the "Questions to Ponder" section at the end of each chapter. You will be amazed to see how the text can challenge your mind.
3. Share quotes and content from the book that strike you on your social networks. Join us in our goal to challenge the norm of division present in humankind. Please include my social handle @yvenerduroseau and the book's hashtag, #Alikeregardless #ThisisWhereitBegan

Enjoy the exhilarating, fun, and wild ride!

Foreword

Yvener Duroseau and this powerful book, *Alike Regardless: This is Where it Began*, are a breath of fresh air in a polluted social justice atmosphere. As an attorney, I have been a fervent activist for social justice, very frustrated with the slow pace of progress and the negativity of our rhetoric.

Black lives have been targeted as inferior, despite centuries of extraordinary accomplishments and contributions to society. "Black Lives Matter" is a slogan, yes, but also a movement that advocates for simple justice, equality, and respect. Social justice and human rights should never be abandoned. Economic inequality and structural racism rob society of stability while leaving millions at risk of poverty and violence. We must always fight for and work together to achieve our basic humanity.

In my world, the legal world, we see multiple examples of racial injustice. Black communities are over-policed and under-protected. Educational tools are often substandard; computers are a luxury. There are huge biases in wealth, housing, employment, and criminal justice. Blacks are ten times more likely to be charged with a crime—over three times more likely to be shot by the police. Sentences for black criminality are 20% higher than those of whites. And, while blacks make up only 13% of the population, they constitute over 47% of the nation's wrongfully convicted and exonerated population.

Mr. Duroseau offers this simple premise: Our petty controversies over race are "a little ridiculous." I couldn't agree more. We face a pandemic, climate change, air and water pollution, an energy crisis, food shortages, global property disputes, weapons of mass destruction, poverty, economic injustice, and multiple other controversies, which threaten our planet and our way of life. Through it all, aren't we more likely to solve the world's problems if we work together? Are we more alike, then we are different? Can't we discover our common humanity and celebrate our diversity rather than fight?

Yvener is someone who might, understandably, have a chip on his shoulder or hate in his heart. Instead, he preaches: "Love thy neighbor." His guiding principle is that we learn to love, respect, and listen to one another, regardless of racial or religious differences. Act in ways that cause the least harm and prioritize peace and love over hate and division. He doesn't suggest that embracing these concepts will be easy, but the survival of humanity is at stake. With so much disinformation floating around cyberspace, in traditional media outlets, and on social media, we must bridge political and ethnic divides to discover and embrace our common humanity.

Yvener's positivity is profoundly contagious. Diversity and love are our greatest problem-solving assets. This soul-searching experience could begin in childhood. Are you being raised in privilege? What is the ethnic make-up of your community? Do you enjoy cultural and socio-economic advantages? Will you use these advantages to continue to elevate yourselves? Or to lift others?

I highly recommend his book to anyone seeking to part ways with a hate-filled attitude. If you are a diversity advocate, introduce this important book for someone who you know is not so inclined. At the very least, educate yourself, try to advance the conversation, set a positive example, and do well by doing good. If we all adopted the demeanor and philosophies of Yvener Duroseau and *Alike Regardless*, the world would be a far better place. If you have the good fortune of meeting Yvener, chat with him for a while. Tell him Mark M. Bello sent you and please give him a huge hug. You will feel better about the experience.

Enjoy this powerful book. Embrace its dynamic messaging and concepts of peace, love, and our common humanity.

~ **Mark M. Bello,** Award winning author, Attorney, Social Justice Advocate

Chapter 1

This Is Where It Began

Along time ago, a large group of people lived on their own. They lived in relative peace and minded their own business. Over time, another group of people, while traveling and looking for free land for themselves, discovered this first group living on their own. Because they had different skin colors and their lifestyles and culture were different, the traveling group made themselves believe this other group were lower humans. So, they invaded the lands of this first group, set themselves up as superiors, and ruled these people. They claimed all their resources for themselves, but they didn't stop there. They bundled the people up and shipped them in terrible conditions to lands miles and miles and miles away from their homes to work as slaves on big cotton farms. Does this story sound familiar?

Well, here's another story:

Once upon a time, one man hated a group of people. He thought he was better than them, believed they were unclean, and needed to be gotten rid of. He hated them so much. He wished they would die. One day, it occurred to him he could get people to kill them. So, he set to work, convincing his people this group he hated so much were responsible for their misery. His people, so convinced, set to work killing so many of those people it shudders anyone to remember. Does this seem familiar as well?

The slave trade and the Holocaust are two famous instances of the cruelty of racism. There are millions of other instances, greater or smaller in magnitude, past and present. We have the ongoing police brutality in the United States to remind us that racism is still as much of a problem today as it was yesterday.

Unfortunately, racism is not the only divide we have created between ourselves as humans. There is also sexism, classism, ageism, ableism, etc. We seem to have managed to build a chasm between ourselves for every facet of human life. Race, religion, politics, and wealth are just a few tools we use to divide ourselves.

And, we may not know it, but we're hurting ourselves by being divided. The cliché saying goes: "United we stand, divided we fall."

Have you ever taken the time to study nature? There is unison in nature. Everything is in sync. The rain falls into water bodies. Water bodies vaporize and form rain clouds. There is symbiosis. The egrets pick ticks off cattle's bodies for food, while the cattle enjoy this as relief from the itchy ticks. This is the original blueprint for humanity to survive together. When we get divided, we do not survive. Even when we survive, we are fractured.

This book was written to challenge the norm of division present in humankind. I mean, look at yourself in the mirror. You have two eyes, a nose, a mouth, two ears. You're breathing, and that's why you're alive. Look at the person right next to you. They have the same features as you too! They're breathing too. Have you looked at a herd of cows before? If you're not a farmer, you could hardly distinguish between them. They all look the same. They're all cows to us; no Angus or Holstein or Hereford to us, just cows. Well, what if I told you that when cows look at us, they can't distinguish between us either? Crazy, right? We're all two-legged creatures to them. No Hispanic or Asian or Muslim or middle class or liberal. Just humans.

It's time we saw ourselves in that light too. At the foundation, when we strip away all the constructs we've built as a society, all we can see ourselves as is human. Two eyes, one nose, one mouth, two ears. Breathing and eating to stay alive.

Have you ever considered that life would be a whole lot easier if we just saw everyone else as human? We wouldn't have to keep up a whole subconscious list of different ways to behave to different people. There would be just one general behavior and just one way of seeing everyone as human. We wouldn't have to keep up with the increasingly complicated guidelines and dictates of political correctness. The point of political correctness only came up because of our divisions and the attendant inequality. Where everyone is treated equally, nobody would feel they are underrepresented or unrecognized or discriminated against. Life would be simpler than we know it. Every one of us was born naked and crying. No one came out of the womb with a religious or political affiliation badge or ideology that one race is better than the other. We're all born equal because we're all created equal. That makes you wonder, why do we grow up to convince ourselves we're unequal? That is where this book comes in, to take us back to our default setting: seeing the next person as an equal.

The divides we have painstakingly built over centuries of living have done nothing but make life a living hell for us. Do you ever feel like burning your TV or phone whenever you listen to or read the news? Because nothing good or happy or hopeful ever comes on. It's either war, or terrorist attacks, or explosions, or racist incidents, or shooting incidents, or sexual harassment incidents, or some other doomsday event. The news makes it feel like the sun doesn't shine anymore and the sky isn't blue anymore. And they're not faking it: these things are happening all around us. Everything going wrong today can easily be traced back to the divides we have built up, the differences between us we have magnified.

We have disconnected ourselves from our common humanity, and it has cost us much. Too much.

In this book, you will learn about these divides. What are they? Why do they exist? What causes them? How do they affect us? What emotions cause us to divide ourselves?

Answering these questions is just as important as any other thing you'll learn.

Charles Kettering once said, "A problem well-stated is half solved." To figure out how to solve a problem, we must first understand what the problem is. Only then can we figure out what the best solution would be. A sickness well diagnosed is already half cured.

It won't be an easy route. Truth learning is hardly pleasant because it will usually involve us pointing our fingers at ourselves as the cause of our own problems. But that process is deeply important. You will learn how to break down these divides by being a better person to yourself. How? You might ask. There is a saying in Latin: "Nemo dat quod non habet." In English, it means you cannot give what you don't have. If you don't love yourself, you will be hard-pressed to do the same for others. If we don't know what we look like, we won't realize that others are just like us.

Therefore, the first step is to improve ourselves inwardly to treat ourselves better. This way, we can express that change outwardly towards our fellow humans. We can break down walls and see ourselves in others. When we have that consciousness of equality, we are bound to treat others better than we already are doing.

I advise you to approach this book with an open mind and heart. Some things you'll read will be drastically different from what you're used to. Be prepared to change your worldview, your way of thinking. Be willing to learn new things and try out those new things.

> *"We cannot solve our problems with the same thinking we used when we created them,"*
>
> Albert Einstein

If we are to move beyond where we are to a better world, we must think and see things differently. We must be willing and courageous enough to act differently because we can't keep applying the same principles and expect different results.

It won't be an easy journey—the hardest thing to do as a human is to change the habits we are already used to. Here, we are talking about deeply ingrained habits that have had centuries to be fine-tuned for easy adaptation. But it is not an impossible task. It helps if we view ourselves as superheroes on a mission to change the world. The superhero never has it easy; the villain is never easily overthrown. But if there's any reason we resonate a lot with superhero movies, it's because good always wins in the end. Apply that same thinking here. However difficult it is, we can win in the end. And what is this end goal? The goal is love. Love trumps hate; therefore, love trumps the divides we have created. Why should I care? You might be asking. Look around you, look inward. The division is hurting us in more ways than we can imagine. Every one of us is in danger of getting hurt just because we differ from others. We must close this chasm; we must get back to seeing everyone as an extension of ourselves. Only in this way can we guarantee our safety and happiness. It begins with every one of us on an individual level.

QUESTIONS TO PONDER...

It is important to know how you feel towards division because your opinion on the matter would, most importantly, determine how you will view the succeeding chapters of this book. Where you stand in all of this will determine how you would treat the matter.

So I ask, do you regard division as an issue at all, or you see it as normalcy thinking that it is the nature of man to be divided?

_____
_____
_____
_____
_____
_____

If you have a contrary opinion, then:

- How do you feel about cases of racial injustice?

_____
_____
_____
_____
_____

- What is your general disposition towards discrimination?

_____

_____

_____

_____

- What is your opinion on the belief that change begins with every individual and that we all have a role to play towards fixing the issue?

_____

_____

_____

_____

- With the matter of concern, in your place, what things do you think you can do, and what roles can you perform?

_____

_____

_____

_____

Chapter 2

Along Came Division

In the previous chapter, we established that a divide exists amongst humans. In this chapter, we will delve deeper into understanding this divide, its causes, and its effects. But, before that, let us first understand why a divide exists. Conflict is an inescapable part of living nature. Wolves go in packs, and you'll usually have one pack fighting the other. Same for lions. One male lion fights off others so it can have the whole pride to itself. You see this in a lot of animals. Even plants try to outgrow each other so they can have more access to sunlight.

Why? The resources for living are limited, whereas the competitors for those resources are a lot more than what is available. In the lawless state of nature, conflicts will arise as living beings struggle to get these resources for themselves. In this state, only the strongest survive, according to Darwin's theory of natural selection.

How does this apply to humanity? Before civil society, humanity lived in that lawless state of nature, where every man and woman lived for themselves. Conflict was, therefore, inevitable in the struggle to survive on the limited resources.

But the establishment of civilization required that we find better ways of resolving these conflicts, by finding ways to ensure that the limited resources somehow get round to everyone or are utilized for collective benefits. Humanity sought ways to multiply the limited resources where they are renewable, such as agriculture. Regulations were brought in place to limit the use of those ones that aren't renewable, like freshwater. If we are in this civilized age now and have found a way around sharing resources, you might say, why is there still so much conflict in the world today? Because of the divide between us. In modern history, none of the wars fought have been centered on the resources needed for living. Nobody fights for food anymore or drinking water. We fight because we are told we are different, and different is wrong and should be squashed. Some fight because the divides put in place deter them from living their best lives. These divides exist because we have lost sight of the foundational fact that we are all humans, all equal, all with value. We have let false beliefs distort our perception of self and perception of others. We see people through stereotypes: we buy into the idea that certain races or classes have certain tendencies. So, when we meet an individual from that race or class, we do not see their individuality or their humanity, we see the stereotype we already have of them, and we judge them through that. We can attribute this to a lack of understanding or forgetfulness.

When we understand that we are equal when we realize that every human life has value, our way of thinking changes, and we are bound to do things differently.

It is not enough to understand this. We must also constantly remember it. When we forget what we have understood, we go back to our old way of thinking and behaving.

To illustrate these points, let us analyze division on a smaller, interpersonal scale. Say two people meet each other at a bar. One is a liberal while the other is a conservative. As they discuss, they realize they have very different views on issues. The discussion degenerates into an argument. The argument gets heated. A fight breaks out. This conflict did not arise out of a need to survive, as in a state of nature. It arose out of the perceived differences these two people saw in each other. They did not understand, or if they did, they failed to remember that they are the same human, just with differing ideologies. If they realized this, there would be no conflict. They would simply acknowledge the difference and move on. When we see others as an extension of ourselves, we are more likely to treat them the way we want to be treated. Nobody wants to be hurt. Nobody wants to be treated badly or differently just because of their skin color, or position in life, or sex, or age, or any other factor that makes them different. At the heart of it, we all want what's best for us. When we understand our common humanity, we also want what's best for the next person.

What Causes The Divide?

We center these divides in our perceived differences based on our race, religion, political ideologies, position in life, sex, age, etc. The Merriam Webster dictionary defines racism as "a belief that race is the primary determinant of human traits and capacities and that racial differences produce an inherent superiority of a particular race." Racism is the belief that people from a race behave a certain way and that one race is better than the other. When we look at people through racist lenses, we do not see them; rather, we see what we believe of their race. The thing with stereotypes is that it gives us a prejudgment of how a person will be, even before we have encountered the person. This is an unfair way to view people. We put the person in a box and deter them from being themselves. They will probably follow the particular trope we believe belongs to their race. Racism is a product of a lack of understanding. We see people whose skin doesn't look like ours, and we don't understand that difference. What we don't understand, we fear. What we fear, we seek to suppress.

Therefore, we divide ourselves along the lines of skin color, and treat badly the races we believe to be lesser than us. Racism is an enduring problem of society today. Children grow up getting racist ideologies instilled in them. They become adults and their default behavior is to view people who don't look like them differently, to treat them differently. Beyond individual expressions of racism, the divide has been ingrained into the structure of society. We have laws that legalize and propagate racism. We have institutions that carry out racist acts. And these can still be traced back to individuals and groups of individuals. Instances of racism abound. The most common in the United States remains police brutality aimed at people of certain races. Black and brown-skinned people are disproportionately at the receiving end of police violence, with the number of people who the police have killed without provocation rising every day, including children and teens.

2020 was rocked with the death of George Floyd, amongst others. Despite prolonged and massive protests following the deaths, police violence is still ongoing. During the Black Lives Matter (BLM) protests sparked by the death of George Floyd, the police displayed inappropriate force against the protesters, many of whom were peaceful. Conversely, during the Capitol Hill insurrection by Trump supporters, most of whom were white supremacists, the police were markedly lukewarm in dealing with the rioters, despite having forewarning on the riots. Racism is the greatest divide humanity struggles with. It pervades all others.

Religion: The weapon of religion has usually been coupled with racism in dividing humanity. Since religion expresses a people's culture, when we look down on a race, we will also look down on all their attributes.

When the Europeans set out to colonize Africa and the Americas, they took their religion with them. They suppressed the religions of the colonized places, which they claimed to be evil while imposing theirs. Sometimes, entire populations were decimated because they were 'pagans'.

Several wars have been fought in the name of several gods. Even today, religious wars are going on in disguise. An instance is the prevalence of Islamist terrorist groups, who believe that their religion is supreme and they have a mandate to kill those who do not believe in it. The religious divide stems from the false belief that the god we subscribe to is the better, or only, god, and every other person who does not believe in that god is wrong or sinful. We forget that a primary thread pervades all religions: equal creation by one god. We are not made by different gods, but one. Our different expressions of that one god then stem from our different cultures and experiences and upbringings. The most ironic situation in life is that religion, which is supposed to be a weapon of peace, has been turned into a weapon of war, hatred, bigotry, discrimination. We have bastardized religion.

Politics: The United States is famously divided between the Republicans and the Democrats. The Republicans hate the Dems and the feeling is mutual. The politicians are always at war in Congress, and we, the masses, follow. It gets worse during elections when friends and family members fight over the singular issue of who one will vote for. We forget that, before politics, we are human first. We forget no one was born red or blue, left or right. We scrutinize political contenders, not on the strength of their accomplishments and manifestos, but along party lines.

Our preoccupation should be demanding the best living conditions from our government, not dividing ourselves with political agendas. When we subscribe to the political divide, we allow ourselves to be used as puppets by the ruling few, whose priority is their best interests, and not the interests of the populace. We are all collectively affected by government policies. We should then focus our efforts on holding the government accountable rather than tearing our eyes over differences in political ideologies.

Thanks to different political ideologies, on the wider international plane, actual wars, trade wars, and other wars have been fought and are still being fought. The West fears and detests communist countries, and the feeling is mutual. Countries have been invaded in the name of liberation from what has been perceived to be 'bad 'political systems.

If we truly have understanding, it wouldn't be difficult for us to figure out that the 'rightness 'or 'wrongness 'of a system lies in the quality of life of its citizens and not in its similarity with ours. Surmounting divides will require our realization we must not police people into being similar to us. We must see the good in our differences.

Wealth: There is the upper class, the middle class, and the lower class. This divide stems from the position of a person in life and society. We turn up our noses on folks we believe we're better than because we drive better cars, eat in flashier restaurants, use costlier gadgets. We forget that we were never born with any of those and won't die with them either. It is not sensible to shame people because of where they are in society. The guy on welfare is just as equal as the millionaire. The woman using food stamps is just as human as the one lunching at a five-star hotel. Wealth does not make a person. Everyone is a human with value, regardless of what they have or what they don't have. Rather than let wealth divide us, we should seek ways to ensure equal distribution of our resources.

Sexism: We live in a patriarchal society that places women directly below men, regardless of race, class, or religion. Women are just not believed to be good enough, and because of this, they have a harder time of all other divides and their attendant effects. They face degradation in the home, office, school, etc.

Before the movement of feminism for the emancipation of women's rights, women were treated as the property of the men they were under, who could be their father or brother or husband. An adult woman was even seen as less equal than a male child.

This divide is what fuels sexual discrimination. The rampant nature of sexual harassment that women face is an offshoot of the mentality many men have, that they are more powerful, and therefore better, and therefore can have their way with women.

The recent wave of feminism has, to some extent, alleviated the situation of women by insisting that women are just as human as men and ought to be treated equally and given equal opportunities. A lot remains to be done.

Ableism: This is discrimination or prejudice against individuals with disabilities, according to Merriam Webster. This goes beyond people with physical impairments to include people suffering from mental disorders. Not enough attention is paid to people who are not heteronormative. Passive ableism is still as dangerous as its active counterpart. Everyone is human, regardless of their disabilities. We divide ourselves along the line of ability, with the disabled usually left behind in our policies and our thoughtfulness. Take parking lots, where abled individuals park in spaces specifically reserved for disabled people. There is not enough access created for the disabled regarding ease of access to buildings, the media, etc. Concerning mental disabilities, not enough effort has been dedicated to understanding mental illnesses and providing adequate help to people suffering from them. The larger society looks down on people they deem abnormal or retarded. This is visible in bullying that children and even adults with special needs receive from able people.

Ageism: The COVID-19 pandemic was devastating to older people. And it opened our eyes to their discrimination in society, with younger people refusing to adhere to safety guidelines to prevent the spread of the disease. Some even went further to call for the deaths of old people expressly. We seem to forget that aging is an inescapable and irreversible natural process and is nothing to shame anybody about. The only right way to deal with age is graciousness. We cannot be young forever. And we cannot expect people of different age groups to have the same tastes. With old age comes a better appreciation of life, something that seems to lack in youth. But we needn't grow old before we can appreciate old people. It is only enough to understand that we are all human, and our age does not detract from that.

In every facet of human life, we seem to have grown efficient at capitalizing on our differences and making them into mountains between us. Our differences are not meant to be grounds for us to discriminate against one another. They help us appreciate one another more, to appreciate the wonder of creation expressed through us. We are each the same, yet we manifest in different ways. That should be celebrated, not hated. We are not robots. That is why we sport so many varieties. Even the herd of cows we look upon as the same, have their differences as well, being of different breeds and sexes, colors, characteristics and disabilities. Yet, they all graze together. They move together in a herd. There is no discrimination.

As humans with much higher intelligence, we ought to do better, yet, we have done much worse than any animal species on Earth in dividing ourselves.

How Does The Divide Affect Us?

Humans are gregarious beings. We are not meant for isolation, but coexistence. When we divide ourselves, we are bound to fail in our efforts to live. The divisions we have mounted between ourselves have cost us a lot, physically and mentally. Rather than give ourselves to growth and development, we are mired in antagonism and backwardness. Even our achievements are not true achievements because our divisions water them down. For instance, developments in health are usually more accessible to certain races and classes. The same with technology. Development that does not favor the entire human race is wanting. War is, perhaps, the most devastating effect of division. Since the beginning of civilized society, countless wars have been fought, countless lives lost, countless destructions brought upon mankind and the planet. We've had numerous conquests on tribal levels, colonization and attendant battles, crusades and jihad, world wars, cold wars, revolutions and insurgencies in countries and regions. And the aftermath of all those is always the same: numerous unnecessary deaths, grief, deepened anger and hate, impoverishment, rubbles where there were once cities, hunger. There is always rebuilding to do after wars. Some take years. Some never happen. People are broken beyond repair. The environment suffers. Scarce resources are used to decimate humanity, rather than to protect it. When you think of it this way, war never makes sense. Yet, our leaders and governments engage in it all too often and with a lot of enthusiasm. Most of it all boils down to ego, and a deep lack of an understanding of our common humanity

War begets war. It does not solve the problem. Most wars are hinged on the egos of the perpetrators. Nobody wants to step down and take the high road. Everyone wants to show their strength, to assert their dominance. In war, there is no place for understanding, for empathy. War strips us of our humanity. That is the only way we can pick up a gun and shoot another person, who is just like us, who is an extension of ourselves.

Beyond the physical aftermath of war, is its psychological effect. War strips us of trust. Nobody believes the other person. Rather, everyone is on guard, ready to be on the offensive at the slightest trigger. That is no way to live. How do we enjoy peace when we do not expect it to last?

On the interpersonal plane, these divides prevent us from achieving the highest level of happiness possible. In a world of divides, there are always those hurt and those who perpetrate the hurt. Neither party is happy. As war begets war, so also does hurt beget hurt. The victim will always seek to hurt the victor and overthrow them. The victor will always seek to maintain their victory at the expense of the victim.

The environment also suffers in a divided world. We maintain our divides at the expense of mother nature. Nuclear weapons and guns and other machineries of war are provided by giant arms industries that pollute the environment. Metals are mined haphazardly to keep the supply high enough to meet the demands. Each year the defense budget of the big countries boggle our minds. In 2020, the defense budget of the United States was a whopping $714 billion. And no country wants to cut down and save the Earth because that would mean giving up their control and authority. Issues that need more attention, like rising poverty and unemployment levels, end up not getting as much attention as they should because we are busy maintaining our divides. We may not know it, but these divides culminate in affecting our mental health adversely. The rate of depression and anxiety has increased exponentially in modern times. More people are dying by suicide than normal. In dividing ourselves, we seem to have ignored how we are linked to each other, how we depend on each other for a fulfilled life. When we isolate and hurt ourselves, we are bound to feel the ripple effect. Fewer people feel happy these days. Even when you feel good, the news comes around and destabilizes you. We are truly alike, which is why bad news about what's happening to another person deeply saddens us.

In more ways than we acknowledge, the divide is doing us more harm than good.

QUESTIONS TO PONDER...

Whether we admit it or not, we have seen this divide working against us some way or the other in the community.

To clarify this, you could pause here and take a quick mental survey of your community.
- What do you think are the main reasons people seem divided there?

_____
_____
_____
_____
_____

- In what ways do you think division has been damaging to development in the community?

_____
_____
_____
_____
_____

- How can this be solved?

_____
_____
_____

As soon as you have surveyed and answered these, you can now challenge your mind with these questions.

- What makes you feel different from another person because of religion, race, gender, or social status?

- What do you think about this feeling?

- In what ways has this feeling affected your relationship with the person or other people who share the same differences?

- In what ways do things that affect others affect you too? If this is not the case for you, why are you not affected by others?

- What is your opinion on the stance that divisions do us more harm than good? What are the reasons for your answer?

Chapter 3

The Motive Behind Divides

Emotions are very strange things. They wield uncanny power that we never attribute to them. We are all emotional beings. Despite all our logic, our actions are still dictated by the emotions we feel.

When we're sad, we make use of the coping mechanisms that we're already used to, even though we might have already thought about it before and decided against it. That's why we go online and shop, even though we've decided to save more and shop less. Or we eat to bursting even though we're on a diet. The divides we have created are no different.

We treat each other differently based on the emotions we are feeling. Let's consider some of these emotions and how they affect our relationship with other people.

Pride: Pride is a tricky emotion. In the Merriam-Webster dictionary, there are several definitions, but two stand out. One is "reasonable or justifiable self-respect." The other is "inordinate self-esteem."

Pride, on its own, is a positive emotion. It never makes us feel bad about ourselves, or we'll never see value in ourselves. A healthy dose of self-confidence is necessary for overall mental health. But it is so easy to overdo pride. When our self-esteem places us on a too-high pedestal, there is the potential that we will be above others. And when we see ourselves as above others, we look down on them.

When we look down on others, we do not see them as our equals. When we do not see them as equals, we cannot possibly be expected to treat them as such. Pride is dangerous because it gives us a false belief, an illusion we are better than others. And we act with this illusion. We treat people condescendingly. We believe we deserve better than others and should get the best things before others.

White supremacy is founded upon pride. This is the belief that white people are superior to other races and therefore should dominate them. It is only pride that would make a person from one race believe they are better than people from other races and should rule over them. This was the foundation of colonialism and the slave trade. The Europeans of the age sought new climes to conquer and dominate because they believed it was their right. They believed they were heads and shoulders above those they conquered. The entire people of Africa were fractured on so many levels because of this. Lives were lost, identities were wiped away, the pride of the people was lost. To this day, the repercussions of colonialism are still being felt in the African continent, with the people struggling to merge their ways of life with those of the Europeans imposed on them, only to come up with distorted products that cannot serve them. An instance is the kind of democracy they practice.

The slave trade was the launching pad for racism. A sad proportion of white Americans are still of the mindset that black and brown people remain slaves and lower people who ought to be discriminated against. Pride is why white supremacists believe the American land is rightfully theirs when in reality, it belongs to Native Americans. They can afford to disregard this piece of information because they believe they are better than the Native Americans and can commandeer their land.

The Nazi propaganda was centered on pride as well. Hitler believed the pure race was the Aryan race to which he belonged. Every other race was impure. He placed himself on such a pedestal he believed he could cleanse the entire world to achieve domination by his perfect race. When you believe you are better than others, you exercise power over them. And if there is one thing history has taught us, it is that unqualified power is dangerous.

Fear: While pride could be a positive emotion, fear is a negative and unpleasant emotion. It stems from anticipation or knowledge of danger. When we fear people, we do not see them as equals. We see them as greater than us in some way and capable of harming us. We fear the danger we might encounter from them. We create a divide between them and us, whether consciously or unconsciously. We either try to get rid of them or get away from them. Fear has the quality of making us irrational. A person afraid doesn't think straight. Have you ever watched a horror movie late at night while home alone? It strikes fear into you in a really bad way. Even though you know too well you're home alone, you entertain the thought that maybe you're being watched by someone or something. You get afraid of the dark and what might be there. You put a torch under your bed just to assure yourself there's no monster there.

Fear makes us make monsters out of others. Often in the U.S., the police have been called on black and brown people by white people for absolutely no reason. Why? Because those white people have been deluded into the belief those people are dangerous and can hurt them and are to be feared. They believe they have a gun and are most likely going to shoot at and rob them. We can see this is an irrational way of thinking, but the fear has been knocked into these people. The Holocaust was founded on fear as much as it was on pride. The Nazis were convinced the Jews were the reason they were in an economic recession, the reason they were suffering. They became afraid and sought to decimate their enemies. Because fear does that to us, makes us believe the other person is the enemy. What do you do to an enemy? You destroy them.

Fear strips us of our trust for one another. Every nation is in a race to amass nuclear weapons because they do not trust others. They fear what other nations would do to them. The point of defense arises from the anticipation of offense. Fear drives our defense policies.

On an interpersonal level, this affects how we treat others. When we're afraid of others getting better than us, we try our best to squash them. Fear informs competition. We make monsters and enemies out of other people, forgetting we're all humans. If the other person is a monster, then surely, we're monsters as well.

Most police shootings of unarmed (and disproportionately black) people arise from their fear of these people, founded on the stereotype they have of these people. Fear puts you on the offensive.

Envy: That feeling you get when someone has something you want, or something better than what you have, you've probably felt it before. Maybe a colleague at work just got a flashy car. Or it's that cool kid in school that has the nicest and shiniest and newest gadgets ever. Or maybe it's the friend of ours with life going so well for them. It's rather a painful thing to feel.

When we're envious of others, there is the tendency for it to turn to loathe. In a secret part of us we don't want to acknowledge, we wish the person would have it just as bad as us, or we wish we can have what they have, or better still, better. With envy, we feel life is treating us unfairly. We're more prone to take life personally, feel threatened by everyone and everything. Envy clouds our sense of gratitude; what we have seems less than it really is. Contentment flies out the window. As we feel the emotion, it fuels our need for self-validation way. We suddenly need to prove ourselves to get to the height we're envious of. We're in danger of being selfish in our quest to get to where we feel we need to be.

Envy builds a divide of competition between us. Our life becomes about proving a point to others, instead of living. A room with envy has bitterness knocking at the door. A bitter person plays the blame game well. And if you play it long enough, you believe it staunchly. You get to where you want to hurt the person you believe causes your misery.

The Nazis are a good example here. The prosperity of the German Jews put them in a mettle. It became easy to blame the Jews for the economic recession in Germany. It became natural to want to hurt the Jews for this. We know the story only too well.

Selfishness: As has been said before, we are essentially social beings. We rely on one other to survive. Necessarily, we ought to look out for one another. However, that is not what is obtainable in our world. Selfishness is preached and practiced. Every man for himself, the saying goes. Selfishness is most pronounced in our consumerist, profit-driven world. Everyone seems to get richer and make profits at the expense of every other person and the planet. 2020 was a year of reckoning for fast fashion companies accused of exploiting native workers in their factories in third world companies. They paid these workers a pittance while overworking them and eventually selling the end products for great profits.

We hear stories of billion-dollar companies exploring their workers with underpayment and bad overworking. They can do this because all they care about is the profit of the company, not the welfare of others.

Selfishness creates a divide of indifference between us. We don't care what happens to others, as long as it doesn't happen to you. We lose our humanity. Selfishness makes us get numb to the suffering of others. We no longer consider the effects our actions will have on others as long as they serve us. That is why we can invade other countries and kill people and destroy lives and properties without a second thought because we believe the benefits of the invasion to us are greater than whatever harm they might cause others.

The reason selfishness does not work is that no man is an island. The action of one person affects another, whether intended or not. When we treat others well, we can have the courage to ask them to treat us well too. The selfish business owners would be wrecked if their workers don't show up for work. They are at the mercy of their workers. Yet, they do not consider this in treating them unfairly. Selfish people hardly consider the duality of being kind. This is because they expect others to treat them well, even if they do not extend this good treatment to others. Selfishness is usually accompanied by pride. The planet also suffers in the hands of selfish people. They believe they will be long gone before the effects of climate change get worse. Therefore, they cannot be bothered to protect the environment to make it habitable for the coming generations. And since their profits are derived from degrading the environment, they go ahead with their actions. Selfishness also drives the divide of class. The wealthy wish to remain wealthy; therefore, they keep manipulating the economic system to ensure their positions and ensure the positions of the lower classes. During the pandemic, the global economy took a blow. Small and medium businesses crumbled or struggled, many people listed their jobs, and inflation reached an all-time high. Yet, in all of this melee, the world's billionaires were making profits and getting richer. This leads one to wonder why there is such a great disparity in wealth distribution, where a chosen few, control the majority of the world's wealth while the disproportionate masses struggle with the remainder. Selfishness maintains the unequal system.

Intolerance: We humans are very different. While we are intrinsically the same, we are yet varied. Whether it be our physical features, traits, and characteristics, beliefs, religion, worldview, political affiliations, gender, sexual orientations, abilities, etc. We are as different as it gets. The problem becomes how we respond to these differences. The right thing would be to appreciate them, as we cannot all be the same since we are not robots. Diversity is a beautiful thing. When we meet people different from us, we have the opportunity to learn. Other people's differences do not threaten us. Instead, they should open our minds to our uniqueness as well and make us love ourselves even better.

Yet, this is hardly the reality we have. Intolerance is the order of the time. When we encounter differences, at first, we do not understand them. It is only natural. Yet, we have a choice, to try and understand, and where that is impossible, to let alone. Yet, the default course of action seems to be intolerance to the difference.

We "can't stand" someone who doesn't dress the way we do, talk the way we do, think the way we do, act the way we do. We try to change them. Where and if that proves impossible, we treat them differently, badly.

Islamic terrorists are incapable of tolerating religion different from theirs, which is why they keep on carrying out their terrorist acts to impose their religion. Neither the Republicans nor the Democrats can understand why the other entertains the ideologies they do. They cannot tolerate that difference and are constantly at war. Those who oppose the **LGBTQ** community cannot for the life of them understand how people can have different sexual orientations or gender affiliations from what is deemed normal. Rather than let it be or try to understand, they embrace intolerance and seek to harm people from that community any chance they get.

Intolerance is the child of a lack of empathy. Empathy requires us to put ourselves in another person's shoes and see the world from their perspective. Where empathy is concerned, we need not have the same experience as the other person. We're required to imagine what it must be like for them, to understand their experience or their decision and perspective.

Empathy asks us to be sensitive to other people. When we understand why people behave the way they do, when we put ourselves in their shoes and admit that we would probably do the same if we were them, we can then tolerate their choices, even if we do not agree with them. We do not have to agree with everybody; we are simply required to give them space to be. Tolerance is reciprocal. When we realize that our decisions and choices also irk others and that we are being tolerated, it becomes easier to reciprocate the gesture.

Hatred: One of the strongest and deepest emotions one can feel is hatred. It comes with anger and disgust at what or who is being hated. Hatred is a powerful and dangerous tool. For the wrong reasons, it can bring about untold destruction.

Imagine buying ice cream on a hot day and getting ready to eat it, only to have someone come around and throw it to the ground. You probably want to drive over the person with a four-wheeler. And you probably will never forget that incident or forgive the person. Right, you hate the person.

Every other emotion above could easily bring about hatred. It is also the worst possible emotion for building a divide. Long-term hatred like the one that maintains the divides we have built between ourselves always feels insurmountable. Racism may have started with pride, but now it is maintained with hate. Centuries of racial tensions in the United States have eroded relations amongst states so much it feels like a permanent fix. Nobody trusts each other; nobody cares for each other.

The North and the South hate each other too, and it's mostly expressed along party lines. Most wars that have been fought and are still being fought are fueled by hate. Nations and factions in warring nations keep trying to outdo themselves in manufacturing horrifying lethal weapons, fueled by hate. We are always ready to go into the next war, never learning from the last one, because the hatred that encouraged the last one has not yet been doused. Countries wield weapons that can singularly wipe out the entire human race. Why are they in existence? The fear that comes from hatred.

If you want to understand what hate can do, read accounts of the torture of prisoners of war. The evil that the human mind is capable of would deeply disgust and terrify you. Hate makes a savage out of a civilized person. Have you ever seen a person convulsed by hatred? It is unsettling to see. The person gets transformed in the most unsettling way.

The reason hatred is the worst possible emotion behind divides is, it feels one with so much energy which they are forced to channel out. And the target is the hated object.

There is a saying by an anonymous person: "What we don't understand, we fear. What we fear, we judge as evil. What we judge as evil, we attempt to control. And what we cannot control...we attack." Most often, our hatred is egged on by our lack of understanding. Did you ever hate math in high school? It was most probably because you did not understand it. We cannot control what we do not understand, and we do not like things out of control. When this is the case, we get frustrated.

Our frustration metamorphoses into hatred. The longer we entertain it, the harder it crystallizes. Then it leaves us with the power and intent to destroy, to feel better.

Our divides do not exist in a vacuum. Humans are intentional beings. We do not simply wake up and isolate ourselves from others. Our actions are influenced by how we feel. Our emotions drive our attitude to ourselves and the people around us.

Therefore, it follows that to change the narrative we are used to, we must begin to change how we feel. We must hold accountable the emotions we let ourselves entertain. Negative emotions not only hurt those we target them at, but they also hurt us too. Hating someone is like holding hot coals in your hands, as the Bible puts it. You think you're burning the other person, whereas you're the one suffering the pain. If we must surmount our divides, we must feel better emotions in place of the negative ones we have grown used to. We will learn how in the succeeding chapters.

QUESTIONS TO PONDER...

We unconsciously wield a negative emotion towards people, get used to it, and then use that to treat them differently. But we can only solve a problem when we know the problem. In the same way, we can only feel better emotions towards others and treat them better if we know what negative emotions led us to ill-treat them in the first place. There, you can provide answers to these questions.

- For what reasons do you look down on people or treat them differently because you feel you are better than they are (if there has ever been a time)?

_____
_____
_____
_____

- Sometimes, it might be treating yourself differently because you feel inferior. If this is the case for you; What makes you fear they are better than you are?

_____
_____
_____
_____

- What do you think about envy being a reason to treat people differently?

_____
_____
_____
_____

- If you have ever found yourself where others treated you differently, and you felt it was because they envied you, what made you think so?

_____
_____
_____
_____

- If you shared the same space with someone who doesn't share the same views with you for a long time, what makes you feel like you can or cannot tolerate such a person?

_____
_____

_____
_____
_____
_____

- If you ever feel resentment towards people who do not agree with your beliefs, how do you express this resentment?

_____
_____
_____
_____
_____
_____

I must commend you if you successfully answered those questions and sincerely. You took a bold step!

The first and greatest step towards fixing a problem is admitting your flaws.

We will learn how we nurse positive emotions towards others in the succeeding chapters and what positive emotions are necessary for fixing the divide.

Chapter 4

Division Is Unfair

Racism is horrible. To be more precise, a division is the biggest enemy of mankind. It does us all no good. This is a fact that cannot be overemphasized. Several prominent people have spoken and written about the disadvantages to racism and the division it breeds but beyond the bad that division breeds, division is unfair. It is unfair to the existence of man he should be segregated based on factors and characteristics not of his own making. Race, for example, is one of the greatest determinants of America's democracy. It determines the candidate who wins the elections, it determines who is winning or losing the end of the policy, and it determines the voters who win at the polls. The history of America has been constantly shaped by division. Although it is constantly developing despite this, the light in which the world is gradually seeing America is diminishing. In speaking of division in America in her graduation speech at the Yale University, the popular writer Chimamanda Ngozi Adichie spoke of a young girl who was given the option to pick a western country away from Nigeria to school. According to her, the young girl's mother had opined that America would be a good place since it has one of the best education systems in the world. However, shockingly, the girl – Nigerian with melanin skin - had blatantly said she would not want to go to school in America because she would not want to die. Apparently, the girl had grown up watching, hearing, and believing that Americans killed blacks based on racism.

We do not need to search too far to find stories of racial injustice. The May 2020 case of George Floyd is evidence enough of what racial discrimination makes us do to our fellow humans. Would anyone believe that a human, because of racial differences, would take another's life? It is painful to even imagine, but it is even more painful that this is a true story, it did happen. The officer knelt on Floyd's neck for over nine minutes and even when the victim kept screaming for his mother and saying he couldn't breathe, his right to life was disregarded by the police officer. What gives a human the right to take away another's life based on race? A life given by the creator and not man.

I want you to take a pause, reflect on what hatred and division have caused, see the monsters it has made out of us, reflect on how a human can disregard another human's life just because they do not have the same skin color, let out a sigh if you want to because this is indeed saddening. Imagine if someone walked up to you and said, "I hate you because you are white" or "I hate you because you are black." Imagine still if your life gets threatened for just simply being you. Yes, preposterous, right? I'm sure Floyd felt the same way, and if at that point he could say more, I'm certain he'd have wanted to ask why they were killing him if it was really because of the counterfeit bill. Even when onlookers screamed for help and paramedics arrived at the scene after Floyd had lost consciousness, the officer still knelt there, pressing the victim's neck. He let the division rule him; at that point, it wasn't just the officer, it was hatred overpowering him.

It is rather disappointing to know there are more stories like this. We cannot act like we are ignorant about the hate with Americans (logically the rest of the world) against the Asians ever since it was discovered that the COVID-19 virus originated in China, a country in Asia. Research has shown that there has been an increase in hate crimes against Asians in the U.S. since 2020. The Corona Virus had been nicknamed the 'China Virus' against this backdrop. So, everyone from China and stereotypically every Asian had been considered a threat to national security. You've probably heard of the Stop Asian Hate Movement. Not that the discrimination against Asian Americans was not in existence before the COVID. This pandemic only saw the increase of this hate, one disturbing incident being the shooting in Atlanta, which was targeted at the people of this descent. We should question ourselves, why would any human go as far as launching an attack on fellow humans? There's no reason justifiable enough.

Racial division or division on any basis at all is unfair, and to further explain why it is unfair is to give room for another side in favor of division the opportunity to give arguments on why division is not unfair. However, these explanations go beyond the questions of 'why'; we also look at the major targets in racial divisions and why these divisions are caused. We make these explanations to understand the psychology of racists better and to put this psychology away. We will consider first the reasons division is unfair.

No two people are born with the same destiny. That implies nobody is born with the same challenge to face. One qualifying nature of every human is that we are diverse in our many experiences and circumstances. Persons are born into diverse unequal circumstances majorly because, majority, if not all of their ancestors or parents were born into such circumstances. Our circumstances are wound up in the circumstances around our parents 'lives and the choices they made or refused to make to change those circumstances, whether or not they accepted their fate or changed it. You could be born into a very wealthy family, another could be born to a farmer, another to a Chinese factory worker, another to poor parents in a place far worse than a slum in India or Indonesia, or to poor families in Haiti.

From the moment we are born, we fight to change our circumstances; however undeserving, belittling or, glorifying we might think it to be. We become more conscious of what others say or are doing to become better. We want to meet up, but we all cannot meet up with the standard, however hard we try. We face a world in which everyone has been asked to get into a race, but some persons have been tied to a pole. Those who are further ahead in the race turn around and ask, "Why are you so slow in the race?" We all cannot compete on the same level with others because of the circumstances of our birth; because of the unfairness in how nature dishes its features on us all. Again, the diversity in our circumstances could be based, not on life's treasures, such as how rich or poor a person is, but on scientific components. Some persons are born to live the rest of their lives battling with one ailment or the other. Others are born gay and then live the rest of their lives, running from society's standards on the existent of persons like them. In some societies, especially in Africa, to be born a female is to spend the rest of your life constantly trying to satisfy the standards and inequality that society has relegated you to as against living your best life.

Nature does not work on sameness: it thrives on diversity. This rubs off on us; no individual, however alike is the same. Therefore, it is unfair to divide persons and cause wars and hatred based on what nature has made normal. It is unfair to say to a child "You should not be here because you are black," or "you cannot go to school because you are a woman," or "your opinion does not matter because you are a pauper." We must understand that the diversity in circumstances is what it is expected to be: this is nature. We cannot all be the same or be born into the same circumstances as to make each other worthy of each other. We must be diverse; and in that diversity, we must find togetherness as against division. Because humans are born into diverse circumstances, they do not possess the same abilities.

No two persons can have the same abilities. This flows from the former. We still come back to humans being diverse in numerous ways. When we create divisions between the human races, we are being unfair because humans should not be expected to possess the same degree of intelligence, professionalism, skills, and aptness. Let us understand the subject of our discussion here: it is not our contention that people should not be separated in light of things they can or cannot do. We are saying here that it is wrong that what people can or cannot do should be the basis of religious segregation, racial discrimination, or political discrimination, eventually breeding wars and hatred. I would expect that a person who refuses to study well to pass his exams to become qualified to become a doctor would not be given the degree (divided from those who will become doctors). We cannot say, "He lacks the intelligence that his mates have to assimilate the sciences needed in studying medicine; let us just help him graduate and not create a divide." No situations are looked at from the aspects of fairness and reasonableness. If a man's abilities or inabilities are not of his doing, then he should not be separated, nor a divide created against him for circumstances not of his own doing. If a man's inabilities (such as his refusal to properly study and assimilate his course content to become a medical doctor) are of his own doing and not that of nature, then separating him from the rest of his folks becomes justified.

When we look at the nature of man as it relates to abilities, we find that certain abilities or inabilities are not of a person's doing. Some persons are born tall, short, handicapped, or blind: all engineered by nature. Again, a man may become skilled in plumbing and another in sewing clothes, and yet another, in drawing houses: all of his doing. Each person picks his path, despite what nature dishes us. These paths further form our abilities and inabilities, separate from those that nature has put in us. When we pick a path for our lives and shape our abilities it would be unfair that we are denied certain social qualifications or hated or discriminated against, not because of the path we have intentionally picked, but because of those that nature has dished us. You should never look down on yourself or others because they possess different skills. Remember, there would be no big companies and institutions without menial labor. And without labor, there would be no economy. Sometimes a great deal hangs on the smallest jobs.

We are all human and it is unfair to create divisions against our fellow humans. The world revolves around humans. We determine the workings of the universe within our control, not animals, not stones, not the sky or the seas. If a man lives with himself (his kind) and not with any other species, why create divisions, race, segregations, spite, hatred, wars against a fellow man? Would we rather live with creatures of the sea or with animals and demons as against our fellow man? The point is this: man constantly creates a division between himself and his fellow man, believing that his fellow man is undeserving to be in the same group or space with him. Who then should be deserving of this space?

That we are all humans and that these divisions we speak of are between humans makes it unfair and important that we point out that we are still all humans. We are still of the same breed - homo sapiens - having one head, the same number of ears, eyes, legs, hands, and having no reason to create a division. We should appreciate our basic similarity and strive to make each other better rather than tear at the already stretched divide.

Who is the Target of a Division?

We have given reasons creating division is unfair to every individual; however, the explanations above will be irrelevant if we cannot further explain who the victims or targets of division are. This is what we shall consider here.

Everyone is a target of a division. No one is excluded from this. Not the President and definitely not the racists and sexists. You and I are both victims of the system we consciously or unconsciously create. Like we had mentioned before, there are diverse and numerous stories of divisions and their consequences. The case of George Floyd comes close. The case of Harriet Tubman who fought tooth and nail to bring an end to slavery also comes close. There is also the case of the Tulsa Race Massacre of 1921, when a white mob attacked residents, homes, and businesses in the predominantly black Greenwood neighborhood of Tulsa, Oklahoma. History holds that a young black teenager, Dick Rowland, entered an elevator at the Drexel building with a white girl, Sarah Page. The girl screamed, making Rowlan run away. He was arrested the next day after it was allegedly reported in the Tulsa Tribune he sexually assaulted Page. The story eventually ended in a war between the white mobs who came to demand for Rowland and the black mob who came to protect their own outside the courthouse. Both groups had acquired weapons.

Also in 1948, a Supreme Court's decision allowed a black family to move into their newly-purchased home in a quiet neighborhood in St. Louis, despite a covenant of 1911 that precluded the use of the house by 'any person not of Caucasian race.'

In Haiti, where I come from, there is evidence of division, especially between the Haitian people and the people of the Dominican Republic. The Dominican Republic had even gone as far as 'building a wall to keep away the Haitians. 'Rights of Haitians are abused and Haitians were even given time to prove their legal citizenship, otherwise face deportation. With this, thousands of Haitians were left homeless with properties seized, physically and psychologically abused. It is hard to think of it now that we were one single island before divisions tore us apart. The root of this division points to Haitian history. The island of Hispaniola, where both people reside, is split into two with Haiti on one side and the Dominican Republic on the other. There was a time when this division was marked with blood from the Parsley Massacre of 1937 which marked the Haiti-Dominican Republic ties. History holds that it was named the Parsley Massacre because at this time Dominican soldiers carried a sprig of parsley around and whenever they saw people who they suspected to be of Haitian origin, they would ask them to pronounce the Spanish word for it 'perejil. 'Knowing that most Haitians would not be able to. Such people were killed and their bodies dumped in the river. With time, even Dominicans that looked like Haitians became subject to these gruesome acts. This particular incident changed the relationship between the Dominicans and Haitians and its effects are still felt in Hispaniola's area until today. But why do the Dominicans hate the Haitians so much? Historically, the Taino people were the primary occupants of the Island of Haiti. They were concentrated on the Island's coastal plains and interior valleys. But contact with Europeans meant conquest. Christopher Colombus so-called discovered the island in 1492 and renamed it 'Espaniola, 'meaning 'little Spain.' This name is what is Anglicized today to be Hispaniola. He returned and established a Spanish settlement, Santo Domingo (what is now The Dominican Republic), under the treaty of Ryswick, to the east of Hispaniola and many more Spaniards arrived on the island. Columbus and the Spaniards deposed the Tainos, exploited and enslaved them to work on their mines and farms, and generally reduced their living conditions. Look how the native people went from 'owners 'to people merely begging to survive. Most died from starvation and diseases and the few who were left managed to mix with other inhabitants of the area. The Tainos were killed and their women were raped. Slaves were also imported from the Caribbean and they faced the same fate. The Spanish were succeeded by the French, who also established their own settlements to the West and imported African slaves to their colony named Saint Domingue. The French didn't treat these slaves any better. Slaves were subjected to the same inhumane acts that Columbus showed Tainos and other Indian groups. Haiti was a French colony. This colony became mixed with African slaves, European colonists and Affranchis (mixed people or free mulattoes). With this existed a hierarchy or class 36 difference. The Haitian society was greatly fragmented. We can see thus, how division existed since this time. The Affranchis, however, who were sometimes slave owners, aspired to be on the economic and social level of the Europeans and claimed to hate a racist society. This sparked a revolution. The French government granted citizenship to the Affranchis, and other Europeans in Haiti were dissatisfied with this. Thus, the country was torn by rival factions, a faction supported by the Spanish Santo Domingo and the other by slaves who rose in rebellion. There was a series of conflicts between the Haitian slaves, colonists, and the British and French colonizers, during which Haiti won her independence from France. But after independence, France never recognized Haiti's independence; rather, she sought to establish a protectorate over her former colony. When Jean Pierre Boyer became president, to unify Haiti and Santo Domingo, he expelled the Spanish from Santo Domingo by annexing it and paying off the French government to surrender Haiti. Boyer achieved unification briefly till Santo Domingo resisted and eventually broke away from Haiti and became an independent Dominican Republic. And up till today, both people are still divided; One Island, yet greatly divided. The division is visible in their interactions with each other. But it is important to look back to our history; only then can we realize that we are one after all. If colonizers didn't come with their notion of division, we would still be one. We've let them play us anyway. Just as they played us then, exploited our land, killed and dehumanize us, we've let them play us into treating 'our own' the same way.

All of us, male or female, white or black, child or adult, religious or atheist, rich or poor are targets of division however little the division might be. These examples might be specific to geographical locations, but the mindset is far-reaching.

Some divisions have far more reaching consequences than others. For example, the division of racism has caused more harm to the whole of humanity than any other division, such as gender discrimination, political discrimination, and religious discrimination. In one division, we further find other far-reaching divides. Even amongst whites, there is further racism such as whether or not one is American or Caucasian, or British. In Africa, there is segregation amongst tribes. People further divide themselves in terms of languages spoken in some parts of that tribe not spoken in some other parts of the tribe. The divide is endless once one divide is created.

The circumstances we find ourselves in determine the division we are target to. In America, a black person would suffer more from racism than would a white man in America or Africa. The division arising from wealth and politics would be targeted more against persons of poor background than any other group. In African nations, certain divisions are suffered more by women; and sometimes, some divisions are suffered more by children. Once we allow any division, either of us can be a target. There is also no limit to the consequences of these targets. I have a personal story to share to show we are all targets of this division. One evening, I went to the Belltower Movie Theater in Fort Myers, Florida, with four friends from high school and there we met a few other girls also from our high school. After the movie, the girls asked us to go hang out in San Carlos Park in their neighborhood. This was a predominantly white neighborhood in south-central Lee County in Florida. When we arrived in the neighborhood, a police officer in the area saw the five white girls with us, the black boys. The police officer said something very humiliating and insulting. I still remember that night when he looked at the girls and told them, "...make sure these guys don't break into any cars...."

Insulting, as I had earlier said. *Did that officer just judge us for being black?* I had wanted to ask. He wrote us off as criminals just because of the color of our skin. The statement he made that night was no different from saying to the girls, "These guys are thieves."

Imagine being wrongly accused of something you never even thought of doing, because we were really just there to hang out.

Sadly, there are so many other young black boys facing this and it isn't just on a racial basis.

A person who is a target of a division could suffer mildly or severely, but the important is that he would suffer. Targets of one divide usually become targets for another divide. The divide and consequences are religions. When people segregate against their fellow man, is there a justifiable reason behind it? Why do people want to put other races or religion or political sections down?

The popular saying," Power corrupts and absolute power corrupts absolutely" is attributed to Lord John Edward Acton. This implies that man, by his very primary nature will always seek ways to get power; he would always veer towards control of his situations and his fellow man. Give him little of this power, then he would seek more, and in seeking more, he veers towards corruption and any other vice that would afford him the power he seeks.

We have not drawn allusion to Lord Acton's quote to tell you that power is a bad attribute, nor is it bad to possess absolute power. We have drawn this allusion to help you better understand, subsequently, that in seeking power, division aids in providing it; it engineers it and gradually makes it easier to attain. Creating division amongst people is the first step to getting a section of the larger divide to your side and ruling over the entire divide. In a white nation, a man who wants power and who feels that a black man would likely take such power away from him needs only to say to his fellow white people, "Why would you want a black man to rule us? They would take over our land and infrastructure and when they have done this, they will wipe us all out, leaving only their kind in the world." A man who is patriarchal and who thinks that a woman is a threat to his getting some power would say, "Why let a woman rule us or be promoted? She is likely to get pregnant anytime and would be restricted from participating actively in the office, or she would be too emotional in how she takes her decisions instead of being professional for the interests of the company."

The story of Adolf Hitler comes to mind here. Before he became the chancellor of Germany, he was obsessed with racism. In his speeches and writings, Hitler spread his beliefs about racial 'purity 'and the superiority of the German race. For him, racism must be upheld, particularly the superiority of Germans, so Germany could one day take over the world and eradicate people who do not look like them. He engineered World War II. What Hitler did was leverage the importance of Germans to obtain more power (absolute power). He made Germany believe that they were the only race that mattered and worthy of living in the whole world. This gave Germans a sense of extreme importance and they were willing to give power (continuously) to the person who maintained their importance over other races. This person was Hitler.

Every time people create division, one of the major causes or reasons of such division is to attain power, as illustrated above. We leverage on division to get power where putting down our fellow man would give us a piece of the cake. We discriminate against blacks or a particular tribe or religion in a society where we know that doing that and doing it well will give us an edge over every other person.

Sometimes also, people create division not so they can get a seat at the table of power but so they can maintain their pride. Being at an advantage or being privileged brews pride and pride gradually blinds a person to certain things. Privilege and pride blind because it is like privilege to blind. People born into certain circumstances just grow up believing that persons without the same advantage as they do should be segregated. This might have nothing to do with power: a man who builds a wall of division might not do it because he wants a seat at the table. He could do it because his conscience and the circumstances of his birth would be hurt if he does not create that divide. A person who is born rich and who has lived off their entire life having things handed down to them as against working for it would be less inclined to appreciate the efforts of the poor person doing all within their power to make ends meet. A person with the advantages of education might be quick to segregate himself from those who do not. He forgets, quickly, that we all are not dished the same piece of the pie in life and that while some people have it all, some people will never have it at all. The implication of this is that he tells himself, "I have acquired all this wealth, education, why let someone who has not been in the same space with me?" It is his pride speaking and not necessarily the need for power. Psychologists say that persons who have grown up being at an advantage most times are less inclined to accommodate those who have not.

Sometimes, the division is caused primarily because of the adverse judgment or opinion formed beforehand or without knowledge of the facts. Historically, the world evolved believing that blacks were less human than every other race and so it became normal to create divisions by making blacks slaves and less human. Du Bois, in his book *The Souls of Black Folks*, wrote that the problem of the twentieth century is the problem of color. He asserted that prejudicial beliefs and notions have greatly fueled racism and it has taken more than a decade to change that and the change is not even over. For America, it took Barack Obama being elected as President of the United States of America in 2008 for racial minorities to increase their standing in most civil rights struggles. Even today, we are still struggling with that prejudice. The prejudice that, because Christianity is the first religion known to man, and as such all other religions do not matter or the prejudice that women are less human and as such should not be given a chance in real life matters and situations other than the kitchen are all numerous examples of what has fueled division amongst us. Prejudice breeds division because we work with facts that are not even verified.

Divisions may also be caused by the inferiority complex of the victim/target of the divide, and the absence of communication. Note that the inferiority complex could be psychological and might have nothing to do with an already existing divide. We are naturally structured to veer towards brightness and as such a child born black amid white people even without being divided against might grow up feeling less human than his white folks. Again, the inferiority complex could be fueled by existing divides, such as a person who already knows that their religion would never be accepted in a place and as such goes into the place feeling less human than his fellow men. The absence of communication breeds a lack of understanding. We grow up thinking that a particular group is unworthy of our circle or attention, but we do not give this group or persons a shot at proving us wrong. The world is filled with persons who do not understand each other or the purpose of existence: that we should live in unity despite our differences.

QUESTIONS TO PONDER...

I am convinced that if given a chance to speak, everyone would have a story of discrimination or division to tell, whether they were victims of this inhumane attitude or merely onlookers.

So what is your story? What cases of discrimination have you been a victim of, a party to, or witnessed?

_____
_____
_____
_____
_____
_____

And on a personal note, how do you think you, as a person, can bring an end to discrimination?

_____
_____
_____
_____
_____
_____

Chapter 5

The Home: Its Roots

There has been speculation about where the divide began. There is no real way of knowing that. However, there is something that cannot be disputed. The home is where the divide mentality begins. The environment predominantly influences the growth and development of a child he or she grows up in. Empiricists are of the strong view that a better part of the development of children is hinged on their nurture in recognition of the nature-nurture argument. Also, parental beliefs can reflect on a child's perception of others. Parents who practice discrimination and are prejudicial based on their social status, religion, tribe, ethnicity, race, color, or other inconsequential societal stratifications pass on these negative beliefs to their children consciously or unconsciously. A parent may forbid his child from associating with children from poor homes, a particular race, or a different religious background. As innocents and in their naivety, children cannot decipher on their own what is good or bad. They pick their values from their immediate environment, which is the home.

Children who grow up in homes surrounded with an abundance of love, care, and affection soon learn to treat those around them in the same way. Likewise, a child exposed to violence, emotional abuse, and parental neglect learns to treat others in such a negative fashion. Children learn by observation and so it is important that at an early stage, they are taught values on what is right and wrong, what passes as acceptable behavior, and how to treat their fellow humans. This responsibility is placed on the parent or guardian with whom they grow up. Several factors contribute to the emergence of divisions from the home and the extension of these divisions.

The relationship between parents and their children is fundamentally important in developing and influencing children's acceptable thoughts, ideas, and behaviors. Where the relationship with their children, individually and as a whole is poor, it may contribute to developing division in the home. Division starts among siblings where parents give undue preferential treatment to a child because they are the first child, or the only male or female child, or where the child is more intelligent than the others. It places an unconscious psyche on the other children, making them feel less loved or inferior to their siblings. Likewise, discussions between parents that occur within the earshot of their children may also create a bad impression on the child. For instance, where the parents constantly make derogatory statements about a neighboring family within the earshot of their children, the children may develop an unconscious belief that since their parents think they are better than their neighbors, then they are also better than their neighbors 'children. Children are simple-minded and do not have the intelligence to filter what they hear and see. It is only at an older age they form thoughts and opinions for themselves. And the way parents treat domestic workers in their employ affects a child's attitude towards others. When children watch their parents maltreat domestic workers such as drivers, cooks, housekeepers, etcetera, they develop the habit of treating people without respect. They grow up with a sense of entitlement and superiority complex towards those who are in positions of service, seeing them as persons doing menial jobs. The parents have either consciously or unconsciously taught their children there is a divide, some sort of class distinction between persons and so they do not find it wrong to treat them without regard.

Children who grow in emotionally abusive environments or broken homes use the infliction of pain on others as an outlet for the lack of love or support from home. A situation is where a child is being trained by a single parent who to make ends meet has to do an undignified job or run so many shifts a day. To deal with the stress of work, he or she takes to drugs and soon becomes an addict. The child becomes a victim of this addiction having to deal with the tantrums and drama of drug overdose. They have to deal with victimization in school and so develop an inferiority complex because they feel less than those who have stabilized homes. Likewise, a child who grows up in a home where the father physically abuses the mother or the children, the lack of a stabilized environment filled with love affects the emotional growth of that child. He grows up with an internal struggle of low self-esteem and strives to fit into society. The consequence of this is that the child would want to make others feel that same way. People naturally project their deepest fears on others and this creates unhealthy division in society. Even when they overcome this struggle, there's still a deep feeling within them they are not enough and they may project these fears on those who work under their employ or with them. This is evident in the way some employers treat their staff, with little or no regard for them.

The media plays a great role in creating division in society. As children, what they read and watch affects their perception of everything. When the child is constantly allowed to watch movies that promote racism, class divides, and general divisions between people, he is exposed to thinking it is okay to treat people in such a degrading manner. Also, in this generation where the internet has taken over the world with everyone having access to all sorts of information, either positive or negative, and with each person left to pick and choose what is acceptable for them, a child is not safe. The media space is filled with a lot of racial slurs and derogatory opinions from persons who are not necessarily experts. This division becomes an epidemic when people view these media influencers as role models unconsciously adopting their views as the standard. Without a doubt, social media continues to be a recognized and welcome source of development in a society, however, the inability of individuals to declutter what they hear and see in this space is a contributory source of division.

What Does Parenting Have to Do with Division?

What we have established is that division begins from home. It is the grass root of any form of division we see in the general public or society. What then is the contribution of parents to this divide?

Our parents are our first world. They are the first faces we see, the first hands that hold us and gradually mold us into the persons we eventually become. As we grow up, they tell us what to do or what not to do. They tell us what or who to play with and what not to play with to not get injured. Our school choices, name, foods, and friends are consciously shaped by what 'Mom and Dad 'would or would not allow. When we make our decisions, we consider the consequences if our parents were to find out. We live out our first teenage years ensuring that we live under their dictates. Put more specifically, the outcomes of children are interconnected within and across diverse spheres of development. This is engineered from the early positive and encouraging interactions of a child with their parents and other caregivers from a little age. What these early interactions do is that they have long-lasting effects on the growth of an individual across their life course, whereby the functions and attitudes of one domain influence the competence of another domain.

By implication, we consciously or unconsciously trust our parents. Whatever they come to tell us, we believe them, knowing it is through their eyes we view the world as what it is. To every question of 'why? 'from our friends as we grow up, we reply, "Because Mom and Dad said so." How we see division is also shaped by our parents. Whether or not we see division as something fair or as something that should exist at all or something that should exist but not in the magnitude in which it exists today is all dependent on the views of our parents as we grow up.

The popular Nigerian Feminist and writer, Chimamanda Ngozi Adichie, said in her short book *Ijeawele* that mothers in Nigeria say to their female children, "You should bend your back well when sweeping because you are a girl." According to her, such a child grows up believing they should or should not do certain things because of their gender. She opines that it attaches a child's ability to their gender and genitals. She preferred that such mothers rather say to the child, "You should bend your back well when sweeping because it makes the floor neater.' "Because you are a girl 'is never a reason for doing something. It is never a good enough reason. To say such to a child as a parent is to create a world filled with the kind of division that relegates women to the house while the only men rule the world. This is a perfect illustration. In reading this book, we see how parents shape the destiny of their kids. We see that whether or not a child grows up feeling inferior or intelligent or strong and undaunted depends on what such a child was constantly told by their parents while growing up. Parents who constantly make their children see that only their religion matters are already implying that mixing with people from other religions is not healthy for them. Parents who tell their female children to stay in the kitchen and make some food and then tell their male children to go into their rooms and read are already implying to one child that education does not matter and to the other that education matters. Parents who constantly turn the side of their lips in disgust at inter-tribal marriages or who constantly talk down on a particular tribe already give the impression that only their tribe and never that of others matter.

In the book *Beyond the Golden Rule* by Dana Williams, she spoke of how her mother said to her on her first day in school, 'You're not any better than anyone at that school and don't ever behave like you are. And no one at that school is any better than you, and don't you ever let them make you believe they are.' According to her, these words introduced the concept of tolerance to her, and starting from when she mixed with people from other religions and class and race, she appreciated that we all cannot be the same and that she must make peace with that and not discriminate against her fellow human. In the same sense, if her mother had told her, in her white skin, she mattered more than every other individual she would meet in her school not of the same color, religion, or class as she was, then she would grow up skewing division in every room, organization or church she gets into. This is what parenting has to do with division.

We look at the case of Adolf Hitler again, the Nazis who believed that the Germans were the only humans worthy of existing. He is known as one of the greatest racists in the world's history and history records that he went as far as killing his son for marrying a black woman. He must have constantly told his children how unworthy of being accorded the role of a human every human being not being a German was. Imagining Hitler as a Father means he would have lived preaching hatred for the opposite religion to his children. He would have said to his wife and children to never be seen around people of color. Contrast Hitler's case with the woman in Chimamanda's *Ijeawele* who was advised to teach her child that everyone matters. To tell her girl child she should not live to be likable to any human on any basis of bias. She should understand that if people do not like her, there would be someone else who does and that if someone she likes does not like her, she must not make herself likable or into something that she is not, to be acceptable. She should remember that she could choose not to like that person too. What we teach our children matters a lot. Statistics show that human psychology is majorly dependent on the teachings and beliefs hewed into them by their parents. It also shows that a grown-up man is more willing to do or not do something if his parents support or do not support him. In most African nations, people's decisions, such as who they should spend the rest of their lives with, are made remembering who one's parents want or do not want. In South Africa, if your parents do not accept your spouse, then your marriage is cursed and it means that your marriage would not be blessed with children.

    This is what parenting has to do with division: any kind of division. It forms it and gives it life. Whether a person grows up encouraging division or discouraging it depends on the parenting such a person was exposed to. It all depends on the words, reactions, and teachings a parent exposes a child to. In all this, encouraging a positive mindset in a child goes Negative way in determining the person a child eventually becomes.

How can bad Parenting Foster Division?

Prejudice is real and refusing to talk about it to your kids is contributing negatively to division. In the book *Beyond the Golden Rule*, Diana talks of a boy who returned from a national parade sad and shouting at his mom about how whites were all racist. The boy told his mother he had encountered a white woman with three children and had mistakenly stepped on her. The woman had glared at him even though he had immediately apologized for stepping on her, she had told her three kids not to allow him to get in front of them. When asked by his mother why he thought the woman was racist and why she had said that the boy had replied, "Some people think all black boys do bad things like steal and fight, so maybe that's what she was thinking about me, but I am not even like that." Sadly, his mother could not argue with his response. As a parent, the first thing to note as a parent is that people will always treat your kids in ways they do not deserve, becoming preconceived notions and prejudice. Teach your children these things: let them know that prejudice is a thing: that it exists. Tell your child that the world is naturally unfair to blacks but there are persons who will be fair to blacks. Tell your child that in certain countries such as India, Portugal, Nigeria, Ghana, and so on, women are not valued but tell her that there are countries where women are valued as much as men are. Tell them that the world naturally veers towards women's being less effective in leadership positions but this is all prejudice. Tell your kids about the history of America. Teach your kids the history of bigotry, sexism and stereotypes, and any form of division that the world faces today. Let them understand that while this is what the world is, it should not define them. If you fail as a parent to talk to your kids about the most fundamental things, they would learn it elsewhere and they would learn it wrongly. By learning it wrongly, they would grow to lend a hand to further divisions, which would further wedge the world into hatred, wars and chaos.

Every child has a sharp sense of what is fair and what is not. Chris Peterson, a positive psychology researcher explains that the absence of fairness in your dealings with your kids gives them a sense you do not value fairness and that they shouldn't either. If in the killings of one religion, a parent says that a particular religion deserves to be killed because they belong to that religion then a parent has failed in teaching such a child the tenets of fairness. Teach a child we all cannot be the same, and in that difference, we should all find what is best for us either as regards religion, class, or decisions. So long as a person's path in life is not unfair, unjust, or harmful to another, a parent should explain to a child that such a path is justified. As much as you can as a parent, help your children perceive your efforts at making life fair for everyone in the family. In making decisions about chores, responsibilities, pocket money, and time, ensure that you are fair to all your kids as well as to neighbors you deal with.

Asides from showing fairness in the family, do something when faced with unfairness. When you witness injustice, racism, bigotry, or stereotypes, take a just stand and challenge unfairness. Teach your child to take action too and to challenge unfairness. Reward your child when they take an unpopular stand when they challenge the existence of division. As your kid's first teacher, model equity. Your actions will always speak louder than your words. When you say that boys and girls are equal but refuse to get your son an Easy Bake Oven because you think it's a 'girls 'thing, you have not modeled your words. You find some division you do not like in your child's school, hold a petition drive, write an editorial in the school's paper or organize a boycott. Do something different and make it count.

A parent's love changes all things, especially in a world such as ours. There are many ways to show love to your kids aside from just saying it to them now and then. Being constantly available for them as well as being warm to them is part of showing them love. There is no more pronounced way of saying to your child, 'you matter 'more than actually stopping whatever you are doing to listen and give them your undivided attention. Statistics show that children who have parents who are constantly emotionally available have a better social and academic life than their peers. When you teach a child love, as a parent, you are saying to the child, 'in a world such as ours filled with division, love matters and, in loving, you understand and accept people for who they are. 'A child who grows up with love would be more likely and open to pour out love into the world than a child who grew up in hatred and bitterness. When our kids demand our attention, we would positively influence them if we give it to them. As parents, we are quick to forget that our kids are not the same age as we are and have not attained the same level of reasoning as we have attained. When they become those private, hormonal, and secretive adolescents, we become snappy and dismissive forgetting that it is a phase we should help them go through smoothly. When we respond to our kids kindly, warmly, we say to them, 'I value you as a person and not as an inconvenient nuisance and I understand how you feel; everyone passes this phase in life. 'When they are down or discouraged, gear them up! Be their strength. A smile, a gentle touch, or warm words would go a long way. Don't let your kids see you as the nagging parent or as the unapproachable parent. Loving them, unconditionally, makes them appreciate love and kindness in the world. This means that in dealing with other people, no matter how different those people might be, they would be more welcoming and warmer and less inclined to brew divisions or hatred or chaos.

As parents, we are humans first. We forget this. We must explain to our kids the struggles that we face as humans. Your children would always see you as 'Mom and Dad 'and they would always expect that you live up to that role. They would want you to be perfect, not cry or make bad decisions, but you must learn to remove this mentality or notion that everyone has of who a parent should be or how they should behave. Talk to them about your struggles. If you are having difficulties getting promoted at work because of your skin color, gender or religion, talk to your kids about it. Don't just let them see your struggles against a division from the angle of a parent but also from the angle of an ordinary person like them trying to live life. When you help your kids understand the human part of you, it is easier for them to be more forgiving and accepting of people's differences. They are more inclined to not fix people into a box of what they should or should not be. They are more inclined to forgive imperfection because they understand that we all cannot be perfect. A child would be more open to people not of the same color as them or have the same religion, views, or gender as they do, knowing they have never been trained to expect perfection from all things. They get this notion from seeing and understanding that Mom and Dad have their imperfections and that they also have their struggles and are not perfect.

I would love to conclude with this chapter activity that includes sessions for both parents and children reading this book because as parents, there are certain beliefs or prejudices we may have passed on to our children and this is true and as children, we believe the things our parents teach us to be true and appropriate. Generations live after each other and this is one cause of the problem that lives with us.

QUESTIONS TO PONDER...

I would love to conclude with this chapter activity that includes sessions for both parents and children reading this book. As parents, there are certain beliefs or prejudices we may have passed on to our children, and this is true. As children, we believe the things our parents teach us to be true and appropriate. Generations live after each other, and this is one cause of the problem that lives with us.

- As a parent, what do you think about believing that your ideas shape your child's (ren) 's?

_____
_____
_____
_____

- Having read this book so far, in what ways do you admit that at one point or the other, you may have fueled the division by the ideas you passed on to your child(ren)?

_____
_____
_____
_____
_____

As a child,

- How do your parents feel when you believe or an idea towards others that differs from theirs, or do you live by sharing their prejudices?

_____
_____
_____
_____
_____

- At what instances have you ever been told that you are or treated differently from others by your parents?

_____
_____
_____
_____
_____

After coming this far, what practical ways do you think you can fix the issue that lies in your own home to reflect in the society, hence trying to fix the divide?

_____
_____
_____
_____

Chapter 6

Love Heals All Wounds

By now, you might be wondering, 'Is division that bad? Isn't there a tiny little justification for not wanting that person to share the same space with you just because of the color of their skin and other trivialities?' Or could the reason be that you might have thought up that they deserve it? That people who do not look like, think like, or act like you deserve to be discriminated against. 'Perhaps that guy that killed George Floyd deserves to be killed too, along with every other white racist. 'This might be your theory, or not. To think this way is human, but it shows we have not amassed enough love to travel this world peacefully. Does division lack love? Yes, it does. In this chapter, you would be made to understand what love has to do with division. Besides this, you would also understand why love is essential in bringing an end to any form of division and the incidental chaos arising from it. We would also answer a fundamental question on who really is deserving of our love. We shall look first at what divisions have to do with love.

What does division have to do with love?

Love is a movement. It is what propels each of us towards one another. It is the eradication of the distance, however huge, between us all. The radical potentials of love are its ability to destroy walls, spaces, fortifications that work to separate us. Historically, man has witnessed prolonged loneliness: the story of the creation of man hinged on the need to not leave him lonely, and it is believed that in community, in living with our own kind and in looking out for them, there is love. Love comes with community. Unless man is constantly hinging on love, man must remember that the war against dehumanization is ceaseless. According to Nelson Mandela, "No one is born hating another person because of the color of his skin, or his background, or his religion. People must learn to hate, and if they can learn to hate, they can be taught to love, for love comes more naturally to the human heart than its opposite." It is our nature to love one another, but we are then born into a world where people have created diverse sorts of divisions and we feel that maybe we should try to fit in one. Over time, we have read about persons who have had to give up loving people around them because of the existence of division. Division in any form has the potential of sapping us of all of the intentionality to love another. Leslie Cobbs thinks that people in interracial relationships give up something, an ease about living, in some ways. By extension, people who thrive on love give up something whenever they love in the face of division. She adds that African Americans in America most especially have to constantly 'think about race 'when deciding who to love or not to love. Statistics show that in white schools, blacks are more inclined to show care and become friends with their fellow blacks than with white people and the same goes for whites being friends majorly with their fellow whites. The reason for this is not far-fetched. In division, people are forced to navigate towards people or entities that would not pronounce that division on them. A Muslim in a society where only Christians are recognized would most likely navigate towards the only Muslims in that society, however few they may be, and be less inclined to mingle with Christians or love them. In such a situation, he feels that Christians threaten his life and security in that society and with such feeling, there can rarely be love.

When we talk of division affecting love, there are secondary effects. Assume that a black, against all odds, decides to settle with a white person and then decides to live in a white country like America. The black would have to live the rest of that marriage double-checking every activity of hers or those of her husband. There is the thought of what your husband's white friends are saying about you, how does your husband introduce you to his other white friends, how does he feel when you ask him to escort you to an all-black people's event? And how do you feel about attending an all-white people's event with him? The prejudice interracial couples encounter from strangers is only one small part of how division shapes their everyday lives.

Whatever division has to do with love does not only end with romantic relationships. Romantic relationships are not the only instances where love abounds. Divisions shape how children show love to their fellow children. It shapes the willingness of one neighbor to show love to another neighbor. Neighborhood divisions are strained and stressful whenever one neighbor has to look out for racial undercurrents in everyday social interactions with other neighbors. Division shapes the willingness to lend a helping hand to someone in distress. At every point when we need to show love or where we think we should choose love above all other things, we ask, 'But, is this really worth it? This person is from another race, religion, gender, or political sect. 'It is what society has propelled into us, division, that may dominate our decisions. This is what we all must understand, love comes to man naturally. However, the existence of division in any form makes it difficult to love. Statistics show that even where division is healthy, such as where a company has divided its workers into different groups to enable quick dispensation of the work of the company, such divisions might eventually breed hatred from one group to another group especially if the latter group is doing extremely well in their duties. When we encourage harmful division, we encourage the opposite of love: hatred.

Having understood the relationship between division and love, we shall now further consider why love is essential to make it a tool for eradicating division. The existence of love takes the existence of fear away; it makes man inclined to take chances on people cast away. As the Bible says in 1 John 4:18 ESV, "There is no fear in love, but perfect love casts out fear; For fear has to do with punishment, and whoever fears has not been perfected in love." This makes sense. Let us cast our minds back to all the examples we have given about Adolf Hitler or the killing of George Floyd, we see that for every person who leverages on division, they lacked enough love and absent love they projected their fears into every individual they came across. For example, Hitler, lacking love, feared that every race aside from the German race was against him and his kind. He projected this fear into his fellow Germans, making them believe that they were the only race worthy of existence and this led to the annihilation of most persons who were not Germans. In Floyd's case, the fear of blacks would be a strong reason the white police officer wanted him dead. But then again, why is love essential?

Why is Love Essential?

We should understand, in this section, that the love we speak of here is not only the romantic kind of love. In all areas of human encounter, love is explored and explained here, and we will link the essential nature of love to how it helps us fight division.

As far back as 5,000 years ago, love has been a major key to the functionality of society. The history of man's relationship with God, for example, shows that for every time that man erred away from God's ways, love was the mending factor. In Africa's jurisprudence, the duties of deities to protect a community and help them live prosperously and peacefully as well as the duty to reverence such a deity are hinged on love. Persons, who understand each other better, hinged this understanding on the existence of love. Love connects the world despite distance, and this is evident in the love of a mother for her child even when both are not in the same space. During interracial, inter-religious, inter-political, or interethnic wars, there have been stories of persons who have still found reasons to love despite being on the other side of the divide. In George Floyd's case, even though George Floyd was black and killed by a white policeman, a fellow white policeman had been willing to testify against his fellow white policeman. The son of Adolf Hitler had still found reasons to love a black woman despite having grown up with a father that had preached racism all his life. In Africa, victims of inter-tribal wars are often saved by persons belonging to the tribe who engineer the war. Love breeds reasonableness, and in just reasons, we are willing to lay down our differences to give another person a chance, to give one person among the hundreds condemned to division, a benefit of the doubt. We say, 'what if this person is different? 'and at that moment, we will take chances on them. Connecting with another divide does not just happen because of love for that set of divides. A person who grows up understanding that all Muslims or atheists are bad would not just at the first instance be willing to take a chance on an atheist. However, if one grows up with love, or if love supersedes the hatred in our hearts, if we have been made to understand the importance of love, then at every point we face a division, we are willing more, to give a chance to the other sect. This is how love helps us connect with others in the face of division.

In love, we find the deepest parts of ourselves that we may not have known to exist. Our level of patience, acceptance of certain norms, perseverance, and level of forgiveness, preferences, tastes, morality, instinctive reactions, and thought processes are all revealed in the face of love. This is revealed considering that we are in a situation we have never been before. Love might not help us lean, always towards eliminating division, however, it would help us know where we stand and this matters a lot. Whether you are all for division or against division, you would understand where you stand and most important, where you should stand when faced with love. A teenager faced with loving her white boyfriend or loving her black girlfriend would soon have to decide whether they are for division or against division. She could be constantly faced with having to decide between her boyfriend or her black girlfriend, especially if the two are not on good terms. This is what love would help such a teenager achieve in this scenario: love would help her weigh her choices and help her decide what is fair and just in every circumstance to do. Love will help her realize how fundamental to the world's existence her origin is, and her skin color. This will help her determine if her desire to satisfy a particular person should be made to outweigh her sense of what is right or wrong. When we say love is a path to self-discovery, it is a path to discovering everything good as against everything evil in ourselves and likely to encourage divisions that could brew wars, chaos, and hatred. Love helps you discover that you could be the one on the other side of the divide and treated with animosity and you wouldn't want to be treated that way. Love helps you realize that if you do not wish to be treated that way, you should not treat others that way or encourage others to treat another that way.

Over time, love has proven to defeat bad habits. People are more willing to do or stop doing a certain thing in relationships because of love for their significant other. If you love a person, you will make sacrifices, change into someone better, be more forgiving, and learn new ways of making that love more pronounced to whoever received your love. Whenever love goes sour, you learn vital lessons: the things you or your significant other did to sour the love will be avoided by you going forward. Through every distress, heartbreak, or pain that could come from loving another, we learn in it. Love teaches you that it does not mean you should stop eating out because you had one bad restaurant experience. You just have to not make the same mistake again.

Dr. Martin Luther King Jr. said that one tenet upon which America was founded is collectivism, love, and welfare. Today, these major tenets have been eroded to a large extent. This is not only in America but in virtually all nations of the world. Besides the division of race, majorly tearing America apart, other forms of division are gradually gaining root from the existing ones. At a time like this, one cannot overemphasize how important love is in reforming our society and returning the tenets upon which our societies were founded. Love teaches us to embrace reasons and fairness and justice as against unfairness and injustice. Love teaches us forgiveness so that even in the face of a division, we learn that we should not do to others what we have gone through merely because their kind caused us pain. Love teaches us that no man deserves to suffer for things or attributes not of their own making. If Mr. A treats B badly because Mr. B is black but when Mr. B gets to treat Mr. A badly because A is white, but does not treat him badly, both Mr. A and Mr. B will both have learned that division and hatred get no human nowhere. We all will be better for it. Love serves as a ship upon which we build our future on. Whatever future you might be building, whatever methods you need to apply to get yourself into that future, whatever ideas and knowledge you might need to scale through, knowing there is always someone to bank on or fall back on is important. Understanding we cannot go through this life alone, no man is an island and neither can any man, solely determine the faith of his neighbor is enough reason to journey this life with all the love we can gather. It helps us against division if we build every relationship on love.

Who Should Be Loved?

"...Teacher, which is the greatest commandment in the Law?" And he said to him, "You shall love the Lord your God with all your heart and with all your soul and with your entire mind. This is the greatest and first commandment. And a second is like it: you shall love your neighbor as yourself. On these two commandments depend all the Law and the Prophets."

Matthew 22;36-440

-ESV

The Bible is the oldest book the world has ever known and this important book recognizes the love of God, first and the love for every individual and neighbor. There is no condition attached to loving a person. There is no precedent in this old book for loving our neighbor on conditions. It is a simple instruction to love our neighbor as we would want another to love us. Every person deserves to be loved. Everyone should be loved. The logic is simple: we would want to know how a person we adore and admire should love us and care about us. The reasons for this are also quite decipherable in that people who love us would go out of their way to make us happy and the larger the number of persons available to make us happier, the happier we will be. Knowing you are better off being surrounded by people who love you will get you through life happier and constantly make you fight to retain a person's love as against their hatred. All that usually matters to us all is someone who understands us, someone who gets us and who we can turn to in all honesty when the entire world around us seems crazy and says with relief, 'You get me.'

When we talk of who deserves to be loved we must not fail to talk about who should give love. Everyone should give love. Give love to yourself first because if you don't, no one will. The world would only treat you the way you treat yourself; so, to be loved, you have to love yourself so much that the world is in awe. Faced with divisions, we are quick to think worse of ourselves and to accept the enemy's description of us. As a black man in America, it is difficult to live through everyday hearing, 'you and everyone who looks like you are failures, Negros, never-do-good, and you are eating off of whites because your lands are underdeveloped. 'It takes a lot to get out of an abusive atmosphere, especially when your enemy is towering over you. In these situations, you must remind yourself, first, that you have as much right to be on earth as anyone else despite skin color, religion, political beliefs, or profession. The same God created us all and has put us all on this same earth and no one has the right to deny you basic rights due to humans in a human setting.

To get through division, reminding ourselves that we are worth every stress of creation put out by God in creating us is important.

Understanding you would not be taken seriously unless you stick your foot to the ground and fight for your existence is what would get us all through division. In loving yourself, you would come to appreciate why a fellow man like you, despite skin color, religion, or political beliefs should also be loved. Remember that you cannot give what you do not have. When faced with any form of division, your understanding of how important you are first would help you appreciate how important another individual is. This would often help you navigate this divided world.

In the discussions on self-love, people have opined that it is the excessive love of oneself that makes it impossible to accommodate another person different from us in any way. Put more directly, the love for one's self breeds division. While this can be true, as seen with Adolf Hitler who loved himself and his people so excessively that he did not think that any other race deserved to exist asides from themselves, this is not love. In loving yourself healthily, you do not seek the annihilation of another. Remember that we explained above that an understanding that people who love us would want to help us or make us happy means we would naturally want to navigate towards very cordial relationships with as many people as we can get into one with. Self-love is never an excuse for division. Real self-love helps us appreciate the need to do away with the division leading to hatred, wars, and chaos.

QUESTIONS TO PONDER...

Yes, that is what love is about, and perhaps you need to have a self-check to see

'Are you truly living in love?'

_____
_____
_____
_____
_____
_____

How about you make an affirmation to yourself now and say:

"Above all else, I choose love. In loving myself, I won't despise another. I choose to love my neighbor just as I love myself".

Chapter 7

Love, The Hard Hill To Climb

Love, that's a big one. I really can't define love, because it's easier to say what love isn't than what it is. Over the years, people have tried to define love, they have even classified it; Agape, Eros, philia, etc. The one we are talking about is Agape love, the unconditional love you can have towards everyone. It is unconditional because it doesn't depend on a reason to exist and it doesn't give reasons not to love. It is a love that has no conditions or preference. It does not see class or statute, neither does it see religion or complexion. It is said to be the purest form of love and is even likened to the love God has for us. This does not automatically mean it is unattainable by us. On the contrary, we have been equipped and even shown an example of what this type of love looks and feels like. We know for a fact that someone has achieved this sort of love; therefore, we are caps and able to achieve it too. Because of this, let us consider things that aren't love and can easily impede our efforts to love each and everyone around us. However, at the top of the list, we have something called indifference. Let us talk a little about indifference. For starters, indifference isn't love; it shouldn't take a shaman to figure that one out, but if you didn't know it before, know it now. Indifference isn't love. When you are indifferent towards someone you could not care less if they walked into the train station, tripped over their feet, and got run over by a train or if they won the lottery and became rich overnight.

Indifference is simply the general lack of interest in a person or thing, it is the lack of empathy or sympathy or generally any emotions towards someone, so you may think, 'I don't hate them so I must love them.' Wrong. You may not hate someone, but you may be indifferent to them which means you don't care if they lived or died today. Are you seeing the picture here? Not caring about someone at all or enough but not hating them. With this attitude, there isn't any way you will be interested in the individual. You would not want to have anything to do with them either. Another thing that can greatly impede our relationship with people is hate. People think the opposite of hate is love; they are not wrong, but they're also not completely right. It's easy to hate people. Every day, someone new gives you another reason to give up on humanity. Across the globe, we hear of incidents that occur because of human greed and selfishness. These events should not even exist, but humans allow hate to fill their hearts and blind them to reason. This hate then creates such events and leads to more people harboring hate in their hearts when they learn about what happened. Sometimes, because these events are engineered by a sect of people, naturally, stigmatization begins. We see all of them in that light without considering how it may be affecting them psychologically and even physically. Not that we should not be careful in our dealings with people, but we should apply wisdom and understand that everyone should not suffer for the sins of a few. We shouldn't even let the hate begin to manifest. It will only grow and eventually blind you to reason and make you do things that shouldn't be done at all. Remember, hate only breeds more hate. It breaks trust and leads to disunity. It makes one unnecessarily suspicious and can even lead to acts of violence against the hated party. I know it isn't easy to love people and if anything, it's easier to hate but the fact remains that for us to achieve a global utopia that exists without segregation or discrimination, we need to get rid of hate and it starts with us. On a personal level. Unlearning hate patterns we have internalized. Even the ones we inherited and have held onto for generations. It is time to begin to grow love. Down with the hate, more love in the streets. Little by little, with conscious efforts starting from us, we will be able to disseminate the hate and let love lead. Then we can help those around us and help them get it right. Eventually, these little personal efforts will reach a global scale of unifying us all. Little drops of rain make an ocean.

Now that we have come this far, let us step back to the basics, self-love and loving yourself. Why should you love yourself? Let's make it personal; why should I love myself, how can loving myself help bridge the divide? Then we will also answer why we should love others and how loving others plays an important role in bridging the divide. It is expedient that we understand these basic principles because they are the foundation and building blocks for loving those around us. We will start with self-love because you cannot give what you don't have. And if you don't understand and have self-love, you could end up self-sabotaging and hindering others effort to show you love and bring you close to them without even realizing this is what is happening because you had no such intentions in your head, it just was a factor of years of conditioning yourself not to receive love or being told, in one way or the other, that you do not deserve this love.

An empty bowl cannot pour, if anything, it can only break or be used to store something, i.e., it can collect. But, we are talking about giving, the pouring if you will. More specifically, we're talking love, tough love, not just the positive affirmations and body positivity, or the good self-image and acceptance but also calling yourself out when you do something wrong. The letting yourself know you should not be doing something because it isn't nice or right. To take corrections from others without seeing them as offensive, we must be able to take corrections from ourselves and understand that people give corrections to help us improve. Mindset is important in dealing with ourselves and other people. We need to put in a conscious effort not to see ourselves as infallible, to avoid creating a destructive or demeaning mindset that doesn't allow for interaction and learning with people around us. It is about finding that sweet zone between rejecting love and being proud.

Bringing it home now to answer the first question I asked, why should you love yourself? I will start by saying this: you are worthy of love. If you doubt me, I know someone who begs to differ. He died just for you, and if that doesn't show you just how much love you are worth, maybe knowing He is a king and God should do the trick.

John 3: 16, *"...for God so loved the world, that he gave his only begotten son, that whosoever believeth in him shall not perish but have everlasting life... ."* Often, we downplay ourselves, tell ourselves that we are not worthy of love, make up things in our head, and even convince ourselves with seemingly good thought-out reasons as to why we are inadequate or undeserving of love. Sometimes it is a form of guilt we cling to that prevents us from accepting this love. Other times, events, and learned circumstances keep us caged in a cold room devoid of love. Whatever it is, know this is not true. Despite what the past may have been like for you, despite the mistakes you have made, you need to know, understand and accept that God loves you and has good plans for you.

Jeremiah 29: 11 says, *"For I know the thoughts that I think toward you, saith the Lord, thoughts of peace, and not of evil, to give you an expected end...." [KJV].* Does that sound like something God would do for someone who wasn't important? Taking time out to make good and perfect plans for you, plans that will be of great benefit to you, guiding your steps, and orchestrating events all around you for your greater good, all the events, both the good and the bad. He knows everything happening to you and He is in control, you just need to trust Him to do you good. That goes a long way to show you just how loved you are. Next, you need to accept and under that people around you love you. The world isn't against you. Definitely, there are people out there that will pick on you without reason and will say and do things out of hate towards you, but that doesn't mean there aren't people who would even risk their lives to make sure you lived. Learning to see the good in people and holding an optimistic view in life can greatly affect your openness to accepting love as it comes your way and eventually dispersing it to the world all around you. I know it's hard to trust people with all that happens now but remember you can be trusted. If you're not, then work to make yourself such a person and then pay it forward by trusting others. Even if someone breaks this trust in the future, don't let it close your mind off to everyone, just be careful but still be trusting. Nothing is easy and nothing is perfect. Some people are still undergoing a lot of learning and they need people to believe in them. Also, love yourself because it's good to love yourself. When you love yourself, you take care of yourself, you nurture yourself. You can do things to take care of yourself to ensure that you are in good health and you are living properly. Eventually, you can translate this self-love to others around you. As someone who has experienced love, you can then carry out the command given to us by God to love our neighbors as we love ourselves. Since you now understand this love, you know what to look out for when taking care of people.

You know how to take care of people because you've taken care of yourself. It allows you to express new levels and understanding of love. Giving meaning to 'love your neighbor as you love yourself'. Self-love is the basis for other forms of love; it allows you, the giver, an opportunity to express what you have learned, internalized, and understood. One of the important parts of Loving yourself is that it includes forming healthy habits that enable you to live a healthy lifestyle to avoid things that can make you sick or put you in danger; even avoiding things like self-harm and self-sabotaging. Once you begin to love you're, you no longer act carefree towards your health, emotional well-being, and general wellness. Your physical, psychological, mental, and emotional health becomes important to you, and you take care to put in the effort to make sure that a part of you is not suffering; be it from negligence or any form of trauma. It is needed so you don't have to worry about cutting short your life on Earth and not fulfilling those things which God has placed you on earth to do. With all that being said, do well to start the journey of self-love today. Remember not to put too much pressure on yourself. If it is something you're not used to, it will take time to adjust to the lifestyle. Cut yourself some slack, take it one step at a time, and don't give up, even when it seems like you aren't making any progress or you're reverting to old ways, just keep pushing. Also learn to surround yourself with positive energy, things that make you happy, and appreciate your life and life. Putting such things together can go a long way to aiding your journey to self-love and supporting you even when it gets hard to love yourself. Remember to take it easy and give yourself a little more love today.

Now that we have self-love down and underway, let's move to the next part of our discussion: Why should I love others? Well, why shouldn't you?

That should be your motivation for doing things for people because you love them. As much as we are prone to doing things from a place of selfishness, doing it out of love produces better results and can greatly improve the way you feel about yourself and the person or people you are putting in the work for. The way you feel about someone greatly determines how you will work for them and how you are willing to and eventually going to apply yourself to situations that can help them. That separates the surface work from the extra mile and deep effort and meticulousness we bring out when we're doing something that is of great benefit to us. When you have good feelings towards someone, they become of interest to you. You want to help them, you want to see them flourish, you want to see them prosper, you want to see them happy and you're willing to go the extra mile. You will do things to inconvenience yourself just to make them happy, you're willing to put in the effort to do things for them not just because you have to or you're supposed to or because you're getting paid to, no, now it is because you want to. It becomes second nature, a desire in you to strive for excellence on the other person's behalf. That distinguishes you when you love someone; you apply yourself to situations to help them, you're on the lookout for them, you are thinking of ways to improve things just to help them. That's why you should love people. If you don't love someone, you might as well not bother because you will do these things haphazardly. It is necessary to love people. That's one way to guarantee you have their best interest at heart, no strings attached, no favors expected. You may get tangible benefits from doing things out of love for people, however, that should not be the motivation to love people else if expected benefits don't come, you are most likely to get angry, irritable, and even hostile towards the person you were offering the act of service to and the poor person has to suffer for something they are not aware of. Take the initiative and take the step towards loving people. Start from those around you, extend a hand of friendship, expect nothing in return, and show a lot of patience. You are all individuals from different backgrounds and walks of life. Let these differences be a common ground to celebrate the uniqueness of each of you and not a means to tear you apart. As you do this, remember to keep your mind open and ready for the challenges and blessings that will come with this new change. Even as you are being patient and learning to accommodate people, don't let them get away with things you are not comfortable with, learn to voice out your concerns and reservations with respect and humility. And again, to help and support people, do not overdo it. It is necessary to know when to stop and let people do things for themselves, that is also a form of love. You don't want a situation where the person gets too dependent and cannot send for themselves on their own.

Being on the giving end of things has a way of 'corrupting' your mind. Keep yourself in check, it shouldn't become an avenue to allow pride to take over. One reason it is so difficult to interact with others is pride. You feel you're better than everyone else, harbor thoughts that always sound like *"I deserve," "I should get," "who is better than I?" "I am not wrong, they are," "why should I apologize?"* Do not be mistaken, it is not in every instance that using such words and phrases is wrong, the issue becomes when it's a constant theme at play. You're always out for blood, feeling like no one else should have something except you, you begin to feel like you are entitled to everything and as such, should get whatever it is you want. It infuriates you to see someone get something you feel you should have gotten, what's worse is when you feel the person doesn't deserve it because they are not 'like you.' Pride is a subtle and slow eater. It can easily manifest without you realizing it, which is why occasionally, you should take a step back and evaluate yourself. Ask yourself why you were angry? Why did you think a person should apologize? Did you harbor ill-fated thoughts towards someone? Was it because of where the person was from? Or how they talk? Do you think you're better than everyone? Sometimes, taking a minute to ask yourself these questions goes a long way to saving you from making deadly mistakes that could cost you in the future without you realizing it. It is natural to want to feel important, but the problem is when you allow this to affect your relationships with people, the way you view and value them, how to address them. Such things automatically cause a rift between you and the people around you. Next thing you know, you're on a high pedestal judging everyone else and no one dares to say a word to you. It is easy to fall prey to pride, learn to put conscious effort into stopping it from happening so you can nurture good, loving, and enjoyable relationships with everyone around you. Remember, the goal is for everyone around you, not just 'some' people, because the moment you start selection, you're putting up a divider, you're causing segregation and you are saying these people don't deserve and shouldn't get the things you offer and that isn't the right thing to do. It doesn't facilitate positive relationships with people around you and it can make people doubt themselves and harbor negative feelings towards themselves, feelings of inadequacy, unworthiness and can even make people contemplate suicide. Remember to always consider the feelings of those around you when you speak and act, people remember things. A random act of kindness can go a long way, even if you don't know how much effect it will have, the person on the receiving end will cherish it forever. You may not remember it, but they will. In the same way, doing wrong to someone will stick and it makes a lasting impression on the individual; about you, about themselves, and about the whole world. So next time, think before you do something because you could be setting a standard for a group of people by your actions and words.

It is also necessary to remember that your actions represent demographics, you may be a young man who helps a lady by holding the door for her at a café, so she doesn't have to fidget with the things in her hand. That one act has created an impression about not just people but men as a whole. These impressions we give people each day can help people in their relations with particular demographics or make them less likely to interact, trust, or even work with the demography. So, remember to let love lead as you live each day. Put yourself in people's shoes and also go the extra mile. Be a little kinder, a little gentler. Do more good deeds, small and big. Despite your gender, learn to see people as family. Treat people as you would like yourself treated. Remember, we are all humans first before we are male or female, before we are black or white, before we are short or tall. Make a conscious effort to be nice to those around you. Pay forward a good deed done to you. Set goals on the number of people you want to make smile in a day. Do your chores without being reminded. Buy ice cream for a neighbor you've never talked to or you don't talk to ever so often. People respond to positivity, everyone likes it, eventually, they'll copy you. Spread the positive vibes to all and sundry without choosing who should and who shouldn't receive the kindness. Treat everyone as equals and humans, no matter what. Love doesn't come easy, it's not just something you say you will do and immediately, a wand magically makes you love, no, love is a conscious effort. It takes persistence, heartache, and lots of heart-wrenching sacrifices. The beginning of it is always difficult, but it does get easier to love. Practice makes perfect. It may not be easy to delve into a world of loving yourself and those around you, but it is easier to make yourself love if you keep trying. You'll begin to pick up some 'tricks,' you'll learn when to stop when to say no, when to put in more effort and when to stay on the sidelines and cheer. it will eventually become like muscle memory for you, you'll love freely and without hesitation. It won't matter what the color of the individual's skin is, or their race or tribe, what language they speak, or if they are male or female. All that you must give will be unconditional love, despite who the individual may be, but before that happens, you will need to learn to persevere through the many obstacles dealing with people and their baggage. Sometimes, throwing in the towel seems like the most reasonable thing to do, you will have very sound and logical conversations with yourself as to why you shouldn't be bothered by what happens to those around you. You may even have seemingly concrete reasons to instigate things to happen to someone, but in those moments, those testing and making moments of your life, you need to search deep within you for the right choice to make. A choice made from a place of love and fairness to all and sundry. Something devoid of greed and hate. When this happens, you will know what the right thing is to do and you will need to draw strength to do the right thing and stick to it. For the greater good of all humanity.

QUESTIONS TO PONDER...

To end this chapter, I have four questions I would love to call 'think deep' questions.

- How often do you show an act of kindness?

_____
_____
_____
_____
_____
_____

- What words would you rather use to express love instead of hurt others?

_____
_____
_____
_____
_____
_____

- How do you feel about limiting kind acts and words to certain people?

_____
_____
_____
_____

- How can you represent love more in your actions?

_____
_____
_____
_____

These are enough to challenge your mind and steer you towards love because it's all we need. I call them 'think deep' because you need to search your heart sincerely before answering them. It's easy to preach love. But the question is, do we practice it?

_____
_____
_____
_____
_____

Chapter 8

You Too, Have Value

Everyone has value. It is not a suggestion but a statement of fact.

Know this and know peace. Everyone created, made, or existing has value. The value of a person is not to be measured or given by you or by their boss or by their parents or by how much work they've done or what they've achieved or how much money they make, no, the value of a person is simply measured by the fact they exist because nothing exists that doesn't have value. Everything in the world made has been or created, everything in the universe that exists is of value. We need to know this. It may be hard to see the value and sometimes the value is clouded by feelings of hate, anger, and jealousy. This may be because of insecurity or a superiority complex or narcissistic personality or even a desire to feel better than everyone else. We start to devalue people; we see them for less than they are, less than they can be, less than they should be because in our head we have reduced them and placed ourselves above on a pedestal and everyone else is below and is seen as people of less value or no value at all. Coming to the understanding and realization of the fact that you are not a standard to judge the value of a person is the first step to understanding that value is beyond just what you give a person. Value is a person existing. Everyone has value because they are alive. For existing alone, you are valuable.

It would be wrong of you to think that someone isn't of value therefore, we need to learn to show people they have value to us. This shouldn't be done from the point of selfishness or from the point of what you can get from them or what they can do for you but more of their uniqueness. Letting them know just how great of a person they are, to you and the world. Show them the person of who God has made them be. These are special ways of letting people know their importance. Everyone is unique, let them know this, teach them not to take value from others but from themselves. Let them draw into themselves. Draw into yourself, remind yourself just how perfect and precious you are. Take pride in your differences, everyone is not and cannot be the same. There is a reason there is the only one you, it is deliberate. Trying to blend into the crowd and stripping yourself of individuality to fit in or feel better about yourself if you can conform to a standard is devaluing yourself. There's a reason we have told and we have diamonds, everything is precious in their stead. You never see your hands wake up one morning and turn to another pair of eyes because they think the eyes are now important, the same way you shouldn't change yourself to something else to find value. As the hands have a role to play that's different from that of the eye, so do you have a role tailored to fit your perfection specifically, you now have to discover it and do wonders. The work everyone plays leads to bettering humanity as a whole, we all just play different roles in the grand scheme of life. And as you understand and accept this, you will need to let people know this too. Don't try to change people to what you want. I am not saying we shouldn't improve or help someone, I am only talking about making someone give up their dreams and themselves just to become someone you think they should be. You need to let yourself know there isn't another of you, there can never be another you, same for others, there won't be another of them. Stop this mindless behavior. Let people live and express themselves. Let them be happy in their skin, accept themselves, accept diversity and culture. Everyone is just trying to be the same by washing off the individuality and uniqueness and trying to conform to a certain stereotype, you know, blend into the crowd, don't be conspicuous. Granted, people fear what they do not understand, this doesn't mean you can't teach them. Man is naturally curious, finds ways to show them the beauty of your ways. Remember to also keep an open mind to the beauty of others. Learn to be flexible and adaptable. This will help you embrace others too and see them as people of value.

 Although sometimes, it can be hard because sometimes this value is hidden. At times value manifests itself in its crude form, it hasn't yet been refined, hasn't yet been shown for what it is, what it could be. It is still as coal there hasn't been the change into a diamond which is why we need to look at everyone with potential. Learn to look beyond what your eyes are telling you. It's like asking for a butterfly baby and being given a caterpillar, if you don't know that caterpillars metamorphose into butterflies, you could get angry and even throw the caterpillar away. Because you don't see the value immediately doesn't change that it is a valuable thing. Sometimes you have to go the extra mile to have improvements done, you need to exercise patience. You have to work on your attitude. The way you see things, how you face situations, what is the mindset you carry. Are you always derogatory and condescending or are you optimistic and pleasant? Fix your attitude and the way you view yourself and those around you. Your communication skill too, the way you carry yourself, the way you dress, the way You address people all should show you see people around you as people of worth. Even when you want to exude your value, the way you look matters. Learn to wear your confidence on your sleeves. You don't have to feel it, be what you want to be. Don't say because you don't have these things now you should hide in a corner. Don't downplay yourself or downplay the people around you because you don't see the things you're looking out to see before you can call someone valuable, mind you, value is not all about what you think it is. Your opinion of value doesn't always hold through. The world does not revolve around you as much as you are an important person. Be aware of the fact that everyone is important. People having their life is good, having things that appeal to them specially. Everyone has a place of influence, a place where they are effective where they bring out skills that are natural to them that have been nurtured. Things that are their things don't and really shouldn't be the same as yours or be something you dictate. Just because it isn't something you would term a thing of value doesn't mean you should downplay it. Everybody should be free to do what they want to do, how they want to do it as long as they're not hurting anyone. Allow people to be happy, free them to do what they want. Allow yourself to be happy, don't let the labels don't let the standard, don't let the figure, don't let the images we see all over the media fool you into a place of depression or feelings of inadequacy. The news carries what they want to push. Everything is from someone's perspective and most times, the pictures are doctored images being worked on, edited here and there then turned into something marketable, something that can sell, something they want to portray as the new trend or expectation and not the truth. This shouldn't be what you use to judge yourself or judge another person or push yourself up to achieve because it isn't always realistic. It is achievable because some people have these things. There will always be some people with these things and these things will keep changing which is why it shouldn't become a standard of judging everyone.

A standard that if not met, you are less than you are or you are seen to be incompetent or not enough. Learn to set realistic goals for yourself, learn to be happy about the little things you have, learn to wake up in the morning, and thank God for your life. Learn to see the beauty of life in the bees and the flowers. Learn to see the value of yourself in your inner strength, the strength to wake up in the mornings when you don't want to, strength to not jump into the road when you're tired.

Learn to see value in the strength to smile even when you're feeling down. Learn to see the value of people in holding the door for the person behind them to walk through, in giving to the poor and the needy. These things are what show the true value of people. It is not about how much money you have; it is not about how much you donated to charity, it is not about your gross income, it's not about the car you drive. Look inward for value. Find this value in yourself and others and learn to look at those around you with love.

Yes, we know the world will always be here judging and rigging the system making it hard, people giving us daily reminders and reasons not to be forward in our thinking. However, these shouldn't stop you from putting your value into use and bringing up the value of those around you. You shouldn't concern yourself with what society will say or let what people will say stop you from doing what is good and what is right. Society has done enough harm by causing us to believe in setting a form of supremacy and making certain things appear undesirable. Letting the same society that has caused issues leading to creating rifts that have caused us to place some people above others wouldn't be the smartest things to do. Instead, let us create standards for ourselves, standards that celebrate everyone in their different spheres of life and achievement without putting down anyone. We need to accept and understand each other for who we are and who we are growing to be.

Everyone has been uniquely and beautifully made by God. There isn't a person on Earth without value, God has made each of us unique and beautiful there isn't a single person on Earth without value and importance. Let us hold onto this and remember it as we deal with people day to day. To get everyone to have a particular way or do a particular set of things, live a particular way, and not be who they were made to be would be to say that God is not wise for creating someone the way He created them. Allow individuality, allow differences to take your rightful place in life. The more you try to change people, the more you force yourself onto them, the more you grow a distaste for who they were originally because that then becomes the enemy and what you're fighting against. If anyone then possesses those qualities or anything the person reverts to their true nature, you become irritated and displeased. This can lead to anger and even as much as you discriminate or make it difficult for these people to live their lives. Allow people to be what they want and open your mind to them. Accept them as they are and see the value in them as it is. Don't try to bend it into what you want or put them into a place you want them to be. Don't downplay people, let them be, and allow the world to grow together in unity and happiness.

QUESTIONS TO PONDER...

Dear readers, re-affirm the truth that you too have value, and so do others.

Suppose you have ever disrespected and disregarded your fellow human. How can you stay corrected and always do right by others from this day?

_____
_____
_____
_____
_____
_____

Chapter 9

We Are Human

Why did God create us, man, in his own image and likeness? Why not the fishes of the sea or the trees or stones? What is the essence of humanity? If we understand the essence of humanity, are we living up to it?

What is the essence of Humanity?

The principal essence of man is to preserve the existence of the entire living race. One cannot preserve their fellow man without hanging on to the dictates of goodness, love, and peace. For every man who exists, he must ensure that he does not exist alone, he must ensure that he is not an island and that he works towards ensuring that his fellow man is preserved in existence as much as he is. This is the primary essence of humanity. Diverse persons have explained this essence of humanity in diverse ways.

According to John Hume, difference is the essence of humanity. The diversity in humans is an accident of birth and it should not be a source of hatred, conflict, or division. The answer to difference is to respect it. In respecting difference, we find peace and peace is a fundamental principle in living through life. Amongst all living things created by God, man is the only entity created in the image and likeness of God. Understanding this presupposes that God, being a personification of love himself, wants us all to reflect his nature in our everyday dealings with our fellow man. Every man we meet reflects a part of God. This does not mean that when we see evil in men, we should assume that God is evil. Instead, we should understand that God needs us, in our imperfect state of sin, to constantly navigate towards being as free from sin and as perfect as he is. He wants us to walk towards being like him. The existence of evil in man presupposes that no man is born perfect; from birth, we already have something to work towards – a nature of goodness that erases the evil we are born with. The essence of humanity is that we all constantly strive towards freedom of our will. This should be based primarily on knowledge of our world and the subjectivity and unity of opposites in nature.

In this essence, man can change his physical, mental, and social existence based on the positive knowledge of the world and of himself, especially as a social being. In this way, he can reduce the contradictions existing between the subjective man and what nature actually is, he can reduce the contradictions between humanity and the world around it, but never really eliminating these contradictions. With a full understanding of the essence of humanity, man is less likely to see the need for a divide. This does not primarily mean that an understanding of the essence of humanity gives him the supernatural power to eliminate any kind of divide. However, he is more likely to create less divide, even if he cannot totally eliminate those already in existence. This is a climax between 'being 'and 'knowing. 'To exist and to know, at the same time what is best for humanity. To know what our real purpose here is.

In the world's oldest book, the Bible, we are made to understand that the greatest commandment for every being is that we love our God, our creator, first, and then we love every man as we love ourselves. This is fundamental. We are not told to simply love our neighbors, rather, we are told that we must love our neighbors. This is why it is called the greatest 'commandment. 'This is one essence of existing, of being, and of being created by God in his image and likeness. This old book does not tell us to simply love our neighbors; rather, we are told that at every point we love our neighbors, we must ask ourselves this pertinent question, 'Would I want to be treated the exact way I am about to treat this person? 'If the answer is in the affirmative, then we should treat our neighbors that exact way, if not, we should think of how we would want to be treated in such situations and treat our neighbor that way. Simply do to others what you would want others to do to you. It then boils down to the fact that if you do not want to be divided against, you are not to divide against your fellow man. This is the essence of humanity, of your living; that you treat others how you would want them to treat you; that you preserve humanity by so doing.

Living Out Humanity

We understand now why God created us and even if we have no belief in his existence, we see from God's perspective and from all we have discussed so far why we were chosen to be in his image and likeness. It is important that we understand our purpose or essence on earth as humans and that we live out this purpose. Living out our purpose on earth means we would be making some intentional efforts at promoting peace in our badly broken world. We give some ideas on doing these few things.

Make a personal commitment to nonviolence. It's easy to become a monster when we have been treated badly. It's difficult to show love when we grow up, knowing we are hated for the harmless decisions we have made or who we have been created into. However impossible this might sound, make it a duty to try as much as possible to live a life of nonviolence. When you do it, and your neighbor does it, and someone else who sees you both doing this, also does it, the world is better off. We all will eventually come to appreciate a nonviolent world.

When you see another in trouble, don't pretend like you do not see them, don't deflate, don't sweep it under the carpet; offer a helping hand. Remember the verse we talked about in the oldest book, about the greatest commandment. At every point we find someone needing help, ask if we would want to be treated in the same way if we found ourselves in the same situation. If we answer in the positive then it is okay to treat such a person that way. Be kind to the world and be kind to yourself.

Show yourself how to take life kindly through deep breathing, through appreciation of what is around you. Take time out to appreciate nature, take a deep breath, take things easy with yourself, and advise yourself like you would do another fellow you love or care about. In doing this, you find it easy to show kindness to another.

It is also important that we constantly talk about kindness. Talk about kindness to someone you think is not kind. It's not enough to show it. In showing kindness to others, try to lend a helping hand to the vulnerable; the homeless, those with physical or cognitive disabilities, the older ones, etc. In dealing with the vulnerable, remember that they would not always want your pity. Deal with the vulnerable like you would deal with a completely capable person needing help. In pitying persons with disabilities, we often remind them of their disabilities, of the things they cannot be or achieve because of their disabilities. We make them live life thinking they have made it that far because of pity as against their abilities or strength. No individual should be treated that way or made to go through life that way.

Be kind, even to Animals. Animals are easily looked over. We say, 'it's just a dog and it should be treated not like a human, 'but we are quick to forget that it is a living thing and that all living things deserve to have their existence preserved. People around us watch us and understand what we attach value to and what we do not attach value to. I know you may be wondering why this should even be brought up. But, in all sincerity, how we treat an animal reflects, however little, how much regard we have for humanity and how far we will go to preserve the existence of mankind. Dogs, cats, monkeys, puppies all have their worth amongst humans, they reflect all that God has made us be, diverse. We cannot all be the same, whether as humans on the one hand or as humans living with animals on the other hand. We should strive in this diversity and keep the world peaceful.

Speak out against prejudice and discrimination when you see it. We talked about this before, however, from the angle of parenting. In our schools, on the streets, in our churches in our mosques or offices, if we see someone being discriminated against on some basis, we should stand up against it. This is much more than doing to others what we would want others to do to us. It is about preserving your sense of what is right and keeping away what is wrong. To bring an end to one form of division or stand against it is to say to the world, 'this is not the best way to live'. We are indirectly making the world see the defects in building a bridge between humanity as against making peace. In speaking against prejudice, we must be ready to have those tough discussions with our friends, acquaintances, our partner, children, and even colleagues at work. Do they have a notion about a gender, religion, race, tribe not totally true? Try to make them understand that they should not condemn an entire set of persons because of what some persons have done. Tell them it is not right to do so. Discuss prejudice and discrimination whenever it comes up. Don't pretend it does not exist or that it is a minor issue or that it is not your business to talk about it. Make it your business. In standing against discrimination, you would have to show others that it is possible to stand against certain discrimination. It is possible to stand up against race in a racial country like America, even as a white man. It is possible to stand up against gender inequality in African countries, whether as men or women. Muslims can marry Christians. Be the change. When people see how genuine you are in pushing forth the change, we all yearn for but cannot bring to reality, they would start, however little to put in an effort. Often, all we need is a push or an example of what our world can be like without division. In light of these examples, there is a greater chance that we could all one day strive towards peace and unity as against division.

Take a deep breath before you speak, whenever you are angry. When people get on your nerves, as they would, count from one to ten, take a deep breath, and then give a less scathing reply. Impossible? You cannot control yourself? Then simply walk away from the situation before it gets worse. Don't talk about it to anyone, just leave the scene. Take some time off and then find someone to talk to about it. It is better to talk to people who care about us and who we can confide in whenever we have been extremely angered. Piling up emotions is a bad thing to do, especially bad emotions. Let it out, cry it out, after leaving the premises that have made you that way. This way, we would be avoiding violence and another possibility of unhealthy division.

Develop a spirit of forgiveness also. Developing a spirit of forgiveness takes more than just reading this book and understanding it. It takes constant practice as well as constantly associating with persons who help you value the importance of humanity around you. Let's do this: whenever someone offends you, or whenever you think someone has greatly offended you, try to take time away and leave the premises as we explained in the preceding point. Ask yourself sincerely if what happened was really about you or if it was about the other person. Talk to someone who cares about you to reach this decision. If you find that what has happened is about the other person, find in your heart some compassion for that person, realizing that such a person might also struggle from the divided world we have all created. It would be best for us all if we regard people who hurt our feelings as our teachers on maintaining a peaceful and less divided world. If you are a member of a religious society, do religion so it unites us all. What do I mean? There is no debate that we belong to different religions or religious groups inside a single religion, but all these groups still teach virtues. Imbibe them! Whatever religion you practice, try as much as possible to reflect the teachings of that religion that encourages the preservation of humanity, one that encourages oneness. For instance, do not come to church and speak to the congregation about how you think persons who attend other churches (that is not your own church) would go to hell. By doing this, you are building divisions amongst the congregation. Do not preach to a family that the woman must always be at home and all submissive to her husband without a mind of her own. Teach the family communism; teach the husband and the wife that for a family to work, both must be willing to submit to one another as the time calls for it. Let your reflection as a faithful follower of whichever religion be one of unity and not hatred or chaos.

About being a servant, it is important also that aside from serving and following, everyone should make it a duty to serve or support committees in our societies that encourage peaceful coexistence.

In doing this, we are merely extending our already existing duty to serve. Some people are constantly working to make our society safer, healthier, and a lot more peaceful. Join these people. Joining them does not mean you sign up for the committee. It could be by contributing to their course or by donating to them or by simply lending a voice to an online campaign they started. Whatever you do, the fence is not a good place to sit on.

And last, we live in an audio world. This presupposes that today, we could have a room full of different people who should be learning from or socializing with one another, but they are all on their phones or laptops. The digital age is not bad; it has brought us all the advancements today, making our life a lot easier. Because of all these, try to have a face-to-face conversation with people, to meet up with them and discuss. Try to meet new people, to say "hello" to people we like even when they are just strangers on the road. Try to comment on people's good acts. Create a nicer and freer world through the way you live life.

If like me, your intention is to truly fix the divide, then make a resolution. Create a list declaring the number of things you intend to change or do to make the situation better and mark them off when you have worked towards it. As long as you do not stop, you are one step closer to fixing the divide.

QUESTIONS TO PONDER...

If, like me, you intend to truly fix the divide, then go ahead to resolve it. Create a list declaring the number of things you intend to change or do to make the situation better, and mark them off when you have worked towards it. As long as you do not stop, you are one step closer to fixing the divide.

This is how your list could look like.

I intend to do better by:

- ✓ Treating people nicely- Because everyone is human and worthy of being treated respectfully.
- ✓ Staying open to accepting/tolerating people's opinions and beliefs- Because it is the only way to live peaceably with others
- ✓ Saying kind words and depicting love in my actions
- ✓ Supporting each other and groups that promote peace
- ✓ Treating everyone equally with a nature of goodness- Because we are alike regardless

Add whatever you think you can do better at that would be geared towards fixing the division. It is a personal resolution, and so it can cover many areas.

Chapter 10

The War Against Hate; A Final Call To Action

I would like to start this chapter by genuinely congratulating you on your decision to do this! I can imagine you've had your doubts and your worries, but you disregarded them and started this journey anyway. You are strong, brave, and very committed if you have been able to get this far. It doesn't matter if you skipped a few pages, what matters is that you are here and making another decision right now. This second decision is by far the most important decision you will ever make and it is the decision to love. It is okay to drop the book and just breathe in. As you take that refreshing breath, agree with yourself that you will not let the knowledge you have gained from this book go to waste. Everything you have learned here is valuable and can cause a monumental shift in your life if you would only allow it. This book was designed with you in mind and its ultimate purpose is to get you from where you were when you started to where you have always wanted to be. The key to knowing is to ask and you have asked. By opening and reading the first chapter, you asked and you devoted yourself to know. Before you finish this book and move on with your life, remember that knowledge is wasted if it is not used properly. All you have to do to gain from the knowledge you have on any subject, especially this one, is apply it.

In the previous chapters leading to this one, we discussed numerous aspects and possible causes of the divide. This divide is anything that hinders proper human interaction and shifts us away from the main focus, which is love for one another and the entirety of humanity. Anything that makes us biased against a person or group can be involved or accredited to that great divide. Divisions are unfair because no one chooses to be born into negative circumstances, or at least what is regarded by the privileged as unfavorable. These lives are formed and pushed into existence without their consent, and most times, divisions are based on factors that cannot be controlled by the people being antagonized. How does one stop nature from making them a born pauper?

Several authors, writers, theorists, great minds indeed, have called this divide many things. Pride, racism, class division, and whatnot. These are all words and concepts that truly describe the state of the world's class system. However, none of these fully encompass the actual nature of the divide. The divide is a concept on its own. It is anything that stops us from loving and treating everyone equally.

There is a huge gap in humanity and it is glaringly obvious. What it is exactly, religion or race, that is hard to decide. How did it come to be? That is impossible to trace. One thing we did put a label on is it's a method of transfer. The method itself links all the aspects of the divide to one another, making it impossible to deny that what divides us isn't the most important thing. The most important thing is that we are divided, even among families and small groups. Everyone is a victim of the divide in one way or the other. Some victims are not necessarily oppressed, but a systematic dislike can only be accredited to a blaring or subdued difference in existing patterns. We addressed a few ways that the need to segregate has been passed from one person to the other, but one stood out and it is widely known. Miseducation is at the foundation. For centuries, from generation to generation, there has been the steady, often undiluted transfer of prejudices and this can easily be pinned on the family. Often, families raise children to mirror the overall image they have sustained for generations. These children are taught to eat and walk and speak like their ancestors to uphold and even promote the family's image. It is no news these children are often taught discriminatory behavior which they practice with diligence from an age where they cannot decide right or wrong for themselves. Sometimes, children grow out of this conditioning and gain independence in their own opinions, but this does not happen very often. Veering from the foundation is rare and when it does happen, it usually does more bad than good. Even if the child isn't directly influenced by its family to be a certain way, the society and environment the child grows up in can shape and define major aspects of his or her character and behavioral pattern. This simply means the neighborhood a child grows up in, the friends they keep, the things that happen in their circles even from a very tender age can influence the way a child develops his or her opinions about the divide. The only thing more treacherous than this divide is the alarming rate of self-hate. Not that it is a concept, because it isn't. Still, so many people walk around beating themselves up about one thing or the other and giving themselves crap about someone who they have never even taken the time to know(themselves). It is easy to walk out and believe in knowing others before you judge them, but are you giving yourself the same chance? Are you being impartial to yourself? This basis lays the foundation for how we see and treat others. Sometimes an inferiority complex can cause us to hate the parts of us we see replicated in others or we could disdain people simply because they don't have flaws as obvious as ours. Sometimes the divide is born and bred in the minds of insecure people and it tears up everything and everyone around them.

In Chapter 7, an important question for self-evaluation was provided. 'Why should I love myself?'

If you need reasons like money and other external and temporary factors to make you feel worthy of love, you need to rethink your self-worth. You need to reevaluate yourself, find the parts of you that are good, not perfect. Good will do just fine for this. Love yourself because of these good bits. Then address the parts of you that are flawed, broken, unworthy, and love yourself enough to work towards fixing them. You are not lovable because you have never been broken. What makes you worthy of love is that every broken piece is still uniquely you. You can always rebuild, redecorate if you will. This is your life and the only way to live it is your way, just make sure you are living!

The Bible, in several scriptural passages, urges us to love our neighbors as ourselves. These include but are not limited to Leviticus 19:18, Matthew 19:19, Mark 12:31. How then can you love your neighbor as yourself if you do not even love you enough? A secret to loving right is never to try to pour from an empty cup. The Bible says we should love our neighbors as we love ourselves. That means you cannot love properly until you have learned to love and appreciate yourself first! This is the basis for every other love, including the love for all of mankind.

Another secret to loving right is to realize everyone has a unique value. That value is immeasurable because every human is uniquely designed. There should be no question of race, religious value, exposure, or other measurements of excellence and difference. Learn to acknowledge people's differences, respect and let it draw you to them rather than push you away! Take pride in your differences. It will not be easy to bridge the divide. It will not be easy to turn a blind eye to ethnic differences, cultural differences, class differences, religious and even moral differences. It will not be easy to ignore all these, but it will be worth it if you keep at it! Earlier chapters have promised you that the world will make this as hard as possible on you. The world will not automatically become better because you have changed. This means you must be a new person in the same old society. You will be tested and tried. Just remember, you cannot change the world, but you can change yourself. We have spoken about everything and nothing and the beautiful shades of something between. Race and divisions and unfairness, all sound so technical and practical, but this book will not afford you the life you desire if you do not practice what you are learning. As a parent, a child, a friend, a colleague, you can influence the people closest to you to see things the way you do. You might not fix the divide everywhere else, but you can work on stitching the fabric at your own end. However little your contribution, it will make an obvious difference when you truly make it your lifestyle.

Often, people make excuses after reading a book like this. They give valid reasons they cannot follow through with the principles shared in the book. Don't be one of those people. I know it will be difficult, I am promising you it will be difficult. Despite that, I am promising you that you will be grateful and you will feel satisfied and happier if you do take this path! Have you ever thought of a world where there was only the human race, no color divisions, or power struggles? A world where we all live and love as one is very possible. It is possible if we all personally decide to put our humanity first. We can bridge the divide if we realize that before everything else and after everything is said and done, we are just human. We are all human. Every divide is caused by a secondary difference taught or observed by the party that considers itself more privileged. If we traded in our secondary comprehension of difference for a primary similarity, we would be a step closer to being whole again.

I am excited and grateful that you have taken this journey and I wish you all the love and courage you will need to keep at it! Don't take the easy way out, that is cowardice, fear, hate, disbelief, sameness. Don't agree to this as your normal. Agree to be better. Strive to be better. You can be the change you hope to see. And if you are, the world will see it too. The world can be the place you have always dreamed it to be, if only you will take that first bold step across the divide! Don't stop trying just because nothing is working. You can make this happen and you will be grateful when you see that shift in your life, your mentality, your environment. All humans are equal, so why did pride and prejudice set in? Why wasn't it addressed earlier? Why has it gone on for this long? Why is power just a tool for oppressing and not lifting those who are different? All these questions will come to mean so much more throughout the journey. You may never find answers. And if you do, they may never be conclusive enough. Don't stop pushing when these answers fail to show up. You can make all of this good. You can make all of this perfect. There is no guarantee that the world will see this from your viewpoint, but I promise you that anyone who takes the right path has already chosen his reward. Feel free to go back to the previous chapters whenever you require a companion. Remember, you and you alone can fix the great divide! You can be the hero in this war against hate.

QUESTIONS TO PONDER...

How has this book been able to change your mind towards division?

_____
_____
_____
_____
_____
_____

What makes you think you've been well-equipped to lead the change?

_____
_____
_____
_____
_____
_____

Dear reader, I would love to challenge you finally with this:

If we all rise and fix the problem starting individually, don't you think the tear would be repaired automatically?

_____
_____
_____
_____
_____
_____

Maybe you should think about it as you close this book! Feel free to go back to the previous chapters whenever you require a companion. Remember, you and you alone can fix the great divide! You can be the hero in this war against hate.

I want to end this book with a poem that I wrote about four years ago. This poem is about how to become the best version of yourself. Chapter eight, "You Too, Have Value." underlines that we as humans should recognize our value regardless of our race, gender, sexual orientation, or social class. I hope this poem will challenge you to recognize that you, too, have value and that you should always strive to become the best version of yourself.

I AM THE BEST ME

I once felt like a shadow,
Seen but not heard
Existing but never there;
Always changing to be different,
Like the clothes that I wear.
A slave to the flashing lights
Click! Click! On the selfie stick,
Fifty snaps before the picture feels right.
Every edited upload a pursuit of acceptance,
Every comment a meal to my starving pride.

But what does it benefit a man
To gain the world with all its fans
And live life, nothing like you were meant to be?
Yielding to the urge to fit in,

With the need for approval like a next of kin.
How could I forget that I am His delight?
No fault in me was found in His sight.
Designed as a masterpiece divine

How could I disremember I am the best me?

My self-worth no longer a hankering plight.

Free from the yoke of Hollywood views

No longer a shadow, now the chief of the light.

In His image, He made of me a child

Beautiful and wonderful

I am the best in my own kind.

by Yvener Duroseau

Bibliography

1. Adichie C.N., *Dear Ijeawele or A feminist manifesto in 15 suggestions*. London: 4th Estate, 2017.
2. Britannica, The Editors of Encyclopedia. "Tulsa Race Massacre of 1921." Encyclopedia Britannica, 24 May 2021.
3. https://www.britannica.com/event/Tulsa-race-massacre-of-1921 Accessed 26 May 2021.
4. Britannica, The Editors of Encyclopedia. "Haitian Revolution". Encyclopedia Britannica, 9 Mar. 2020,https://www.britannica.com/topic/Haitian-Revolution. Accessed 26 May 2021.
5. Britannica, The Editors of Encyclopedia. "Taino". Encyclopedia Britannica, 8 May, 2020, https://www.britannica.com/topic/Taino. Accessed 26 May 2021.
6. Darwin C., *On The Origin of Species*. London: John Murray, 1859.
   Du Bois W.E.B., *The Souls of Black Folks*. New York: Dover Publications, 2012.
   https://www.quora.com/Why-are-humans-born-in-such-unequal-circumstances
7. https://www.universityofcalifornia.edu/news/how-race-shapes-who-wins-and-who-loses-us-democracy

8. https://www.washingtonpost.com/news/worldviews/wp/201 5/06/16/the-bloody-origins-of-the-dominican-republics- ethnic-cleansing-of-haitians/?outputType=amp

9. https://www.europarl.europa.eu/doceo/document/E-8-2019- 000947_EN.html
https://www.nbcnews.com/news/amp/ncna1261257

10. https://www.nationsonline.org/oneworld/History/Haiti-history.htm#:~:text=In%20exchange%2C%20France%20rec ognized%20the,weighed%20heavily%20on%20future%20g enerations.

11. Keegan, William F., "Destruction of the Taino" in *Archaeology.* January/February 1992.

12. Williams D., *Beyond the Golden Rule; A Parent's guide for preventing and responding to tolerance and prejudice.*Alabama: Teaching Tolerance, Southern Poverty Law Center

Acknowledgement

First and foremost, I offer my praises and thanks to God the Almighty for His showers of blessings throughout my writing to complete this book successfully.

My heartfelt thanks to my wife, Kimberly, for tolerating my incessant disappearances in my home office. *"Poupée, thank you for putting up with me throughout this arduous process of writing my book."* I can truly say a lifelong partner makes both the journey and destination worthwhile.

I am also grateful to my mentors, Dr. Jean G. Mathurin and Mr. René Godefroy, for always supporting me in my journey. Both René and Jean helped me train the growth mindset I needed for this book to become what it is.

I owe an enormous debt of gratitude to detailed and constructive comments on marketing and promoting my book: Jessica Moronto, Shouberte Jean-Baptiste, Jean-Max Voltaire. They freely gave their time to discuss great techniques to promote the book on social media.

I'd also like to thank Brandon Vassol, who did the audiobook for the book; his voice is an amazing gift.

Thank you for picking up my book. I hope you've enjoyed it. More importantly, I hope it has opened your mind and heart and changed your worldview, your way of thinking as it relates to humankind.

I encourage you to buy a copy for a family member, a friend, or a co-worker.

To stay connected with me, visit my website: WWW.YVENERDUROSEAU.COM

Made in the USA
Columbia, SC
26 September 2021